Tennis Made Easy

Essential Strokes & Strategy for the Modern Game

Luke,
Great improvement this year.
Stick with it,

Good Luck

Kelly G.

Tennis Made Easy

Essential Strokes & Strategy for the Modern Game

BY KELLY GUNTERMAN

NEW CHAPTER PRESS

Tennis Made Easy is published by New Chapter Press (www.NewChapterMedia.com) and distributed by the Independent Publishers Group (www.IPGBook.com).

ISBN – 978-094-2257-717

The cover photo is courtesy of Cynthia Lum.
Internal photo credits are as follows; Page 1 photo courtesy of Kelly Gunterman; Page 4 photo courtesy of Cynthia Lum; Page 5 photo courtesy of Ralf Reinecke; Page 6/7 photos courtesy of Kelly Gunterman; Page 8 top left photo courtesy of Ralf Reinecke, others courtesy of Cynthia Lum; Page 9 photos courtesy of Cynthia Lum; Page 10/11 photos courtesy of Cynthia Lum; Page 12 top row photos courtesy of Ralf Reinecke, bottom photo courtesy of Cynthia Lum; Page 13 photos courtesy of Cynthia Lum, except for bottom right photo courtesy of Ralf Reinecke; Page 14 photos courtesy of Cynthia Lum except for top right courtesy of Chris Rogers; Page 16 photo courtesy of Cynthia Lum; Page 18 photo courtesy of Ralf Reinecke; Page 19 photo courtesy of Cynthia Lum; Page 20/21 sequence photos courtesy of Lance Jeffrey; Page 22/23 sequence photos courtesy of Lance Jeffrey; Page 24 top photo courtesy of Cynthia Lum and bottom photo courtesy of Ralf Reinecke; Page 25 photo courtesy of Ralf Reinecke; Page 26 photo courtesy of Cynthia Lum; Page 27 photo courtesy of Cynthia Lum; Page 28 photos on top left and top right courtesy of Chris Rogers, photo on bottom right courtesy of Cynthia Lum; Page 29 photo courtesy of Cynthia Lum; Page 30 photo courtesy of Chris Rogers; Page 31 photo courtesy of Cynthia Lum; Page 32 top photo courtesy of Chris Rogers (check) and bottom two photos courtesy of Cynthia Lum; Page 33 photo courtesy of Kelly Gunterman. Page 34 photo courtesy of Cynthia Lum; Page 35 photo courtesy of Chris Rogers; Page 36/37 photos courtesy of Lance Jeffrey; Page 38/39 photos courtesy of Cynthia Lum; Page 40/41 photos courtesy of Lance Jeffrey; Page 42 photos courtesy of Cynthia Lum. Page 43/44/45 photos courtesy of Cynthia Lum; Page 46 photos courtesy of Cynthia Lum. Page 48/49 photos courtesy of Cynthia Lum, Page 50/51 photos courtesy of Cynthia Lum. Page 52/53 photos courtesy of Lance Jeffrey; Page 54/55 photos courtesy of Cynthia Lum; Page 56/57 photos courtesy of Cynthia Lum; Page 59 top photo courtesy of Cynthia Lum, bottom photo courtesy of Kelly Gunterman; Page 60/61 photos courtesy of Cynthia Lum; Page 62 photo courtesy of Cynthia Lum; Page 64/65 photos courtesy of Lance Jeffrey; Page 66/67 photos courtesy of Cynthia Lum; Page 68/69 photos courtesy of Lance Jeffrey; Page 70/71/72 photos courtesy of Cynthia Lum; Page 74/75/76/77 photos courtesy of Lance Jeffrey; Left photo on page 78 courtesy of Cynthia Lum, other two photos courtesy of Ralf Reinecke; Page 79/81/82/85/86/87/88/89; Bottom left photo on page 90 courtesy of Chris Rogers, others courtesy of Cynthia Lum. Page 91 photo courtesy of Cynthia Lum; Page 92 photo courtesy of Ralf Reinecke; Page 93/94 photos courtesy of Cynthia Lum; Page 95 photo courtesy of Ralf Reinecke; Page 96/98 photos courtesy of Cynthia Lum; Page 100/101/102/103 photos courtesy of Cynthia Lum; Page 104 photo courtesy of Kelly Gunterman; Page 105/106/107/108 photos courtesy of Cynthia Lum; Page 109 photo courtesy of Kelly Gunterman. Page 110/111/112/113 photos courtesy of Lance Jeffrey. Page 114/116/118/120/121/124 photos courtesy of Cynthia Lum; Page 125/126/128 photos courtesy of Ralf Reinecke; Page 129 photos courtesy Cynthia Lum; Page 130 photo courtesy of Ralf Reinecke; Page 131/132 photos courtesy of Cynthia Lum; Page 134/135 photos courtesy of Ralf Reinecke; Page 136 photo courtesy of Cynthia Lum ; Page 137 photo courtesy of Ralf Reinecke; Page 138 photo courtesy of Chris Rogers; Page 139 photo courtesy Cynthia Lum; Page 142 photo courtesy of Cynthia Lum; Page 143 photo courtesy of Ralf Reinecke; Page 145 photo courtesy of Chris Rogers; Page 147/148/149/151 photos courtesy of Cynthia Lum; Left and bottom photos on page 152 courtesy of Chris Rogers, top photo courtesy of Cynthia Lum; Page 153 photo courtesy of Chris Rogers; Page 154 photo courtesy of wikicommons.com; Page 156 photo courtesy of Cynthia Lum; Top photo on page 158 courtesy of Chris Rogers; bottom photo and photo on page 159 courtesy of Kelly Gunterman; Page 160 photo courtesy of Cynthia Lum; Page 161 photo courtesy of TournaGrip; Page 162/163 photo courtesy of Kelly Gunterman; Page 164/165 photos courtesy of Babolat; Page 166 photo courtesy of Cynthia Lum; Top photo on page 167 courtesy of Kelly Gunterman, bottom photo courtesy of TournaGrip; Page 168/170/171 photos courtesy of Cynthia Lum; Page 172 photos courtesy of Amelia Island Plantation; Page 174/175 photos courtesy of Cynthia Lum.

New Chapter Press would also like to thank Bill Mountford, Ewing Walker, Kirsten Navin and Manfred Wenas for their help with this project. Thank you to Annie Coghill on behalf of Babolat and Kevin Niksich on behalf of TournaGrip for their special efforts with these photos.

Cover & book design by Kirsten Navin.

Printed in Canada.

For my Mother and late Father,
Joan & Tom Gunterman

Contents

Introduction

ALL TENNIS INSTRUCTION IS BASED ON SOMEONE'S OPINION. THIS HAPPENS TO BE mine. You may or may not agree with some or all of the instruction written in this book but give it a chance. There are a lot of years of trial and error in these pages and a lot of help from my friends.

I have been very fortunate in my tennis career, having had the opportunity to work with some of the best teachers in the game. I was also very privileged to have had some great coaches -- Frank DeSantis, who got me started in Bremen, Indiana and Dennis Emery, who gave me an opportunity to play for Austin Peay State University. I have learned the foundation of my profession working with them and it has unquestionably helped in developing my teaching philosophies. While running my own tennis school for the past twenty years, I have been fortunate to work with many terrific people. Through them, I have learned a great deal about tennis, teaching and people in general. To all of them, I am grateful.

This book has been written to help the novice and intermediate-level players improve their skills. The instruction is simple and straight forward. I am always trying to remember that less is more and that keeping the game simple is the key. The goal of the game is quite simple; hit the ball over the net and into the court one more time than the other guy. It is an important concept to not over think your approach to improving your tennis. It is, after all, just a game. Everything takes time. As you look to improve your strokes, don't try to bypass the simple fact that learning to do anything well takes some time and considerable effort. This may sound contradictory but it is simple and it takes work to improve. That is where the greatest satisfaction happens.

Most of all, enjoy the process. Learning is pleasure. Win or lose, you can enjoy this great game for a long time. My friend Bernie came to me at the age of 75, eager to learn to play tennis. Now at 91, he is still an active tennis player and a great friend. He is just one example of tennis being "a sport for a lifetime." As you learn new parts of the game, it will seem like an onion, as you peel away a layer there will be another and another that will keep your interest for a lifetime of improvement and enjoyment.

Stay fit, hit lots of balls and remember the journey is the gratifying part of the process. Tennis is an enjoyable way to get great exercise as well as a friendly way to compete. Don't fret too much over a win or a loss; you can always play again tomorrow.

Kelly Gunterman
2010

Grips

THERE HAS BEEN A LOT TALKED ABOUT, WRITTEN AND TAUGHT ABOUT HOW TO HOLD the tennis racquet when making a particular swing or shot. I'll put my spin on it, clarifying the advantages and disadvantages of each grip and how they influence your stroke and how the contact point must change to adapt to the grip you use. The way you grip the racquet should be what is most comfortable to you. You may want to make small adjustments in your swing to make your grip work better for you. I have found that making a change in your grip is challenging when you have played for a significant period of time.

There are four key forehand grips – each of which have specific pluses and minuses. It is important to understand each of them and how they affect spin and how the contact point must change with each grip. Especially with the forehand, your swing style is an important factor in determining how best to hold the racquet.

It is true, the proper grip is important but it is more important to have your grip fit the way you swing the racquet!

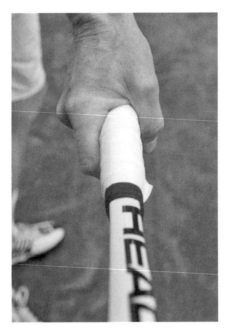

Continental Grip

This grip is also called the hammer grip for the mere fact it is exactly the grip you would have on a hammer if you were to drive a nail. Just hold your racquet as if you were going to drive a nail with the edge of your racquet. The V formed between your thumb and first finger is located on the top of the handle of the racquet. This grip is used for serves, forehand and backhand volleys as well as overheads. It allows you to play all of these shots with the same grip. Though it may be used to hit a forehand, I don't recommend it as it is unreliable and difficult to hit with spin or pace. However, this grip makes hitting with underspin and very low balls much easier. It will also be the grip of choice when hitting drop shots.

Eastern Forehand Grip

This old standard grip was at one time called the handshake grip. Simply place the palm of your dominate hand on the face of the racquet and slide your hand down to the grip. The V of your hand, between the thumb and forefinger, moves one bevel to the right, from continental for right-hand players. This grip is comfortable and very versatile making it easy to change from the forehand grip to a one-handed backhand grip. The tendency here is to hit the ball flat with a lot of power making the shot harder to control. A disadvantage of this grip is that higher balls are harder to hit. It is not the best choice for hitting with extreme topspin.

Semi-Western Forehand Grip

From the eastern forehand grip, turn your hand one bevel of the grip farther under (or behind) the racquet for the semi-western grip. The V of your hand is on the side bevel of the handle. This is certainly the grip of choice for most players on the pro tour, allowing them to hit with power and topspin. Also, it is easier for high-bouncing balls and gives a higher margin of error over the net. As with all grips, the more extreme the turn, (the more to the right and underneath the handle you move your hand), you must hit the ball much more in front and higher. The disadvantage of this grip is the lower the ball, the more difficult the return. It can also make changing grips for the backhand a bit more difficult.

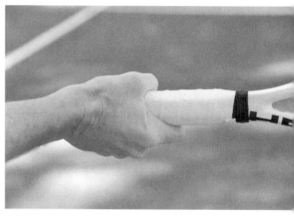

Western Forehand Grip

This grip is quite popular with clay court players to compensate for higher bouncing balls. The western forehand grip is one more bevel to the right from the semi-western. With this grip, the contact point is closer to the body and much, much earlier. Therefore you hit with extreme topspin but with some loss of power. Remember, as we add spin, we lose speed (but more on that later). High-bouncing balls are much easier to handle but lower balls are much more difficult. Also, changing your grip to the backhand side is a lot more difficult because you have to move the grip farther around the handle of the racquet. This grip is usually for clay court players and definitely not a grip to use while playing at the net!

Here you can see, even the top pros can't agree on which grip is best. The variance in grip position will affect the angle of the racquet face through the shot. Notice how all of the players keep their eyes focused forward in the preparation phase of the swing.

The One-Handed Backhand Grip

You will want to find a grip that keeps the wrist in the strongest position with the face of the racquet perpendicular to the court at the point of impact. For right-handed players, the V on your hand moves to the left of continental one bevel. This positions your hand almost on top of the racquet. The proper grip allows you to turn the racquet face down or closed in the backswing allowing for the most topspin. Alternatively, you can open the face or turn the hitting face up in the backswing for more underspin. For most one-handed backhand strokes, this grip of choice allows for a quick and easy shift in grips while hitting a variety of spins. The major disadvantage of this grip is the high-bouncing ball to your backhand. Because topspin is difficult to hit, the slice backhand is a great alternative for balls that bounce above your shoulders. As with the forehand, some players take this to the extreme by moving the V of their hand to the back side of the racquet. Similar to the extreme forehand grip, high balls are easier but lower balls are more difficult to hit.

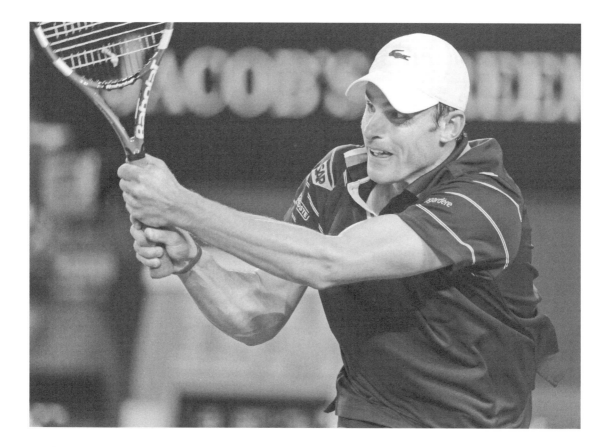

The Two-Handed Backhand Grip

The principal advantage of the two-handed backhand is that you do not have to change the grip of the dominate hand. Simply put the non-dominate hand on the racquet above the dominate hand; in essence you use two eastern forehand grips. Keep both hands together, so that the hands work as one unit. If you are right-handed, the left hand dominates, driving the racquet through the ball. This grip feels much stronger allowing you to hit the backhand with two hands instead of one. The security of having more strength at the point of contact makes it easier to hit, particularly for the novice player, sometimes easier than the forehand. The downside of this grip is your ability to reach balls hit by your opponent at angles wide to the side of the court. If you are more comfortable with two hands and you can hit 90 percent of the balls more easily, you can make a stab at the other 10 percent by reaching for the wide balls with one hand. This one-handed shot must be hit high and deep, buying yourself some time to get back in the point. Another bonus is the added stability of the second hand will allow most players the ability to hit a much stronger return of serve.

Volleys

AS YOU PICK UP THIS BOOK AND START THE LEARNING PROCESS, YOU MAY WONDER why I started with the volleys rather than the more traditional groundstrokes. I have always felt that it is easier to learn simple skills first. When hit properly, the volleys are the simplest shots in the game. As we progress, we begin adding to our skills and exploring the more intricate parts of the game. Also, as we get older we may play more doubles if we're not already. With this information, you will have a leg up on your peers and you can develop as a doubles player.

Virtually everyone begins their tennis education by learning the groundstrokes from the baseline. This makes a great deal of sense since a player employs the forehand and backhand strokes from the baseline more than any other shot. Every player must establish a solid foundation as well as a certain amount of confidence before advancing to the more nuanced aspects of the game. All of us have found the net intimidating during our initial forays in its direction. However, with proper technique and practice anyone can feel comfortable at the net. Even if you are the most enthusiastic baseliner, coming to the net is exciting as well as a productive skill in our development as a tennis player.

When developing your skill at the net, the fundamental rule is to keep everything simple. The less you do with your body, feet and hands, the more effective your game. Remember that all you actually do is re-direct the ball that comes to you. Adopting the correct angle on your racquet face for a particular situation will ultimately result in the success of your shot. With a firm wrist and a little shoulder turn, the volleys are quite easy and a lot of fun. Do not let yourself be misled by Roger Federer or Serena Williams when they take a big swipe at a volley; they practice and play those shots many times on a given day. We mere mortals need to remember the mantra: "Keep It Simple".

When moving toward the net, avoid rushing. As John Wooden, the great basketball coach from UCLA, once said "move quickly but don't hurry." This adage applies to the en-

tire tennis game but especially to the net game. Work your way in methodically and stop when your opponent hits the ball. A good rule of thumb is, when you have hit the ball and it is moving away from you, move in. Conversely, when your opponent hits the ball, stop, usually with a split step or check step. (We will have more on that later.) This maneuver allows you to keep your balance and to change direction cutting off your opponents shot.

This may sound a bit confusing but it isn't. Quite simply remind yourself that "less is more."

PRACTICE DRILL:

To develop the skill of hitting volleys with limited shoulder turn, try hitting reflex volleys with your partner without moving your feet. Starting with you and your partner about 10 feet from the net on opposite sides of the court, hit volleys back and forth without moving your feet. This isolates your upper body eliminating the shoulder turn. Most club players move way too much when playing at the net. Remember this is only a practice drill. I am not advocating not moving your feet when you play but it is a very effective practice drill.

PRACTICE DRILL:

Starting with your partner on the opposite service line, start a volley rally and each time either of you hits a ball, take one step forward. Continue moving forward until you are both very close to the net hitting the ball very softly. How you hit the ball will change as you move forward, driving the volley from the service line to a very soft touch volley when you are both close to the net. This is a great exercise to develop touch and learn to change the speed of the volleys.

Fundamentals to Successful Volleys

○ Stay off your heels and move forward to make contact with the ball. Staying up on the balls of your feet allows you to move to the tennis ball in an aggressive style of play. Try holding the racquet with a continental grip, discussed earlier. This will allow you to hit serves, forehand volleys, backhand volleys and overheads all without a grip change or just a minimal change.

○ Think no shoulder turn. By moving your racquet to the ball, your body will turn enough. A big shoulder turn automatically puts the racquet too far back and results in a swinging volley or, even worse, hitting the ball well behind your body. If you have played tennis for a while, you probably learned to hit the groundstrokes first and to turn your shoulders. Now playing at the net, we must unlearn that move and progress directly to keeping the racquet in front of our body. It is okay to develop a bit more of a turn on the backhand, since you are reaching across your body with the racquet.

○ Think catch. Imagine your partner throwing a ball to you and you catching the ball with

your racquet hand. I'll bet you don't turn your shoulders to make the catch. Have your practice partner throw balls to you with some higher and some lower and see how your hand moves to adjust to the height of the ball. Now, with the racquet back in your hand, hit a few balls while thinking catch. This positions the racquet head for a successful volley.

○ Adjust the racquet to the level of the ball. For low balls, drop the racquet head and open the face of the racquet. If the ball is high, keep the racquet head up through the shot.

○ Squeeze the last three fingers on the grip of the racquet hand. This keeps the wrist very firm. We all have experienced the floppy wrist or slapping of the wrist to hit a volley.

○ "Drive" the racquet through the point of impact. Try to avoid the old thinking of punching the ball. This to me implies hitting and pulling back. By pressing/driving through the ball, you keep the face of the racquet on the plane of the ball resulting in more control and more power.

❍ To feel more comfortable with the direction of your volleys, press the palm of your racquet hand at your target on the forehand volley and the knuckles of your hand at the target on the backhand volley. On the two-handed backhand volley, press the palm of your non-dominant hand toward the target. Keeping this in mind makes directional control of the volley simple and the recovery much quicker.

❍ After hitting your volley, move back to the ready position. On the balls of your feet, prepare for the next ball. Quick feet on the recovery add to your prowess at net. The faster you recover, the more quickly you will be ready for the next shot.

❍ Keep the volleys very simple. This is the most important aspect of learning to volley or becoming a better net player. Always keep in mind, less is more. The fewer moving parts there are, the less chance of a malfunction.

Remember: A good net player is always trying to be more aggressive. Moving in on the volleys opens up the angles of the court, giving you a lot of options for the direction of the shot. More on this later.

Myth Buster: Keep the racquet head above the wrist. This works only if the ball you hit is above your waist. Adjust the racquet head to be on the level of the ball. If the ball is hit low, you must lower the racquet to make solid contact with the ball.

Specialty Volleys

Low Volleys: Let's get out of the old school thinking of keeping the racquet head above your hand. It just does not work on volleys below your knees. Let the racquet head drop; tilt the hitting face of the racquet open toward the sky. Keep your wrist very firm by squeezing the bottom three fingers of your hand on the grip. You do still have to bend your knees, not at the waist and get low for the ball.

High Volleys: Keep the racquet head up through the entire shot, as if you are closing a shower curtain. If you pull the racquet down as you come through, the ball will go in the net. Again, keep a firm wrist and keep your head up through the shot.

Volleys right at your body: Any ball that is hit directly at your body is difficult. Adjust by simply swinging your elbow out and hitting the shot with a backhand volley. Anyone who hits with a two-handed backhand volley may have some difficulty with this shot. It requires you to release the non-dominate hand and make the shot with one hand.

Half-Volleys: This is not a shot of choice but of necessity, usually a result of poor positioning or a tough shot by your opponent. If you are caught in no-man's land and the ball is hit toward your feet, don't panic! Stay low through the shot, shorten your backswing and keep a firm wrist by squeezing the grip with the bottom three fingers of your racquet hand. Direct the ball over the net with an abbreviated follow through. Your goal on this shot is to stay in the

point and make your opponent hit one more ball while you have a chance to move in to a more aggressive part of the court. Think of making the transition from defense to offense.

Drop Volleys: Now we're getting somewhere! We are gaining confidence at the net and starting to develop some touch. The drop volley is the one exception when playing at the net where you will soften or loosen your grip when you make contact with the ball. This results in the face of the racquet rolling under the ball, imparting a great deal of underspin. Imagine hitting this shot so it will land on top of the net. With the backspin, the ball will stop short with little bounce.

Lob Volleys: This shot is exactly what it sounds like, a lob that is hit from a vol-ley. Keep a firm wrist (which we have talked about), open the racquet face and make an exaggerated follow through up and through the shot, as if you were lifting the ball over your opponents head. Stopping the racquet will result in a short lob that can prove to be dangerous. This is especially effective when all four players are at the net in a doubles situation.

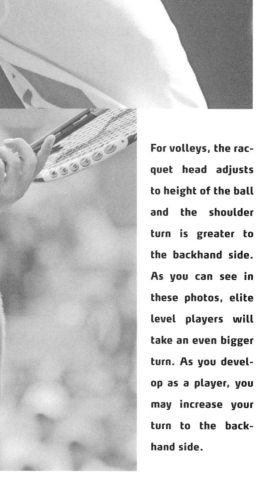

For volleys, the racquet head adjusts to height of the ball and the shoulder turn is greater to the backhand side. As you can see in these photos, elite level players will take an even bigger turn. As you develop as a player, you may increase your turn to the backhand side.

Consistent with all good volleys is focus forward and early contact with the ball. These photos show the need for more shoulder turn on the backhand volley. The following page shows the good extension through the ball.

Overheads

THE OVERHEAD SMASH IS FEARED BY BEGINNERS AND RELISHED BY ADVANCED players. What is the key to making this shot more satisfying for all levels of play? Position! Your position in relation to the approaching ball makes all the difference in this point-ending stroke. For most of us, the stroke is relatively easy but getting in the proper position to make the shot is the challenge, but also a necessity.

The Four Steps to a Great Overhead

1. Drop the right foot back for right-handed players to get the hips and shoulders side-ways to the net. This allows you to slide or side step forward or back to be in position as if to catch the incoming ball with your non-racquet hand. If you are in position to

catch the ball with your free hand, then you are in the proper position to hit an effective overhead. Avoid moving back facing the net, as it is easy to catch your heel and fall backwards. Furthermore, you won't be ready when you do get to the ball because you are not sideways.

2. Place your racquet hand next to your right ear for right-handed players. This prepares the racquet for the shot. Getting in this position early allows you to make subtle changes in the swing. By having the racquet in what has been called the "back scratch position" allows you to hit up and through the ball.

3. Swing the racquet up and through the ball. This motion is very similar to throwing your racquet at the ball. It is also very similar to an abbreviated service motion. If you make contact slightly in front of your body, you can swing much faster and follow through to the opposite side of your body resulting in a powerful, easy-to-direct overhead.

4. Practice, practice and more practice.

If you are tired of dealing with the opponents who seem to lob incessantly, the overhead smash is the answer. With a powerful overhead in your arsenal of shots, it discourages even the most fervent lobbers.

PRACTICE DRILL:

While your partner hits lobs to you, try to literally catch the ball in your non-dominate hand. This helps you to get in the proper position. Remember to prepare the racquet and get your body side on to the net with a good solid "drop step."

The Swinging Volley

This is an aggressive shot, which is meant to conclude the point. This will usually be hit on the forehand side with the same grip you use for a forehand groundstroke. First you should get your feet set. Make the back foot your base similar to your forehand ground-stroke. Keep your head still as you make the swing through the ball. A common mistake is to look at the court in the middle of the swing, pulling out of the shot. Make the swing as if you were hitting a groundstroke and swing through the ball with a full finish. Con-tact for this shot should be made between your waist and shoulders and in front of your body. Go for it. This isn't meant to be one of your high percentage shots, but with some practice and no fear of missing the shot, it can be a lot of fun to hit. After hitting this shot, follow the ball just in case your opponent makes a great return.

Groundstroke Fundamentals

LET'S FACE IT, THE WAY THE GAME IS PLAYED HAS CHANGED A GREAT DEAL OVER THE past 25 years. Take a look at the pro game and you can see just how much the groundstroke game has evolved into big, fast-swinging strokes that generate a lot of spin and power. Many of these changes can be adopted into your game as an active club-level tennis player. I encourage some of the changes and discourage others. Some look very familiar to those of us who have played for a while, others may look a little strange. Keep an open mind and give these ideas a chance. With some practice, these changes can take your game to a whole new level.

I encourage novice players to challenge themselves. Try what would have been more advanced techniques in the past, like an open-stance forehand. I know how hard it is to learn something one way and later un-learn that skill only to re-learn it another way. I feel the un-learning is much more difficult than learning it right the first time. So why not learn it the best way first or at least make the effort to improve your technique? For intermediate players, making these adjustments adds power and consistency to your game.

Keep in mind when learning a new skill, you may have to take one step back in order to take two steps forward.

Let's take a minute to talk about spin. Newer players to the game may be confused with what I have written about spin. We will talk more about this as we progress into the groundstrokes.

Topspin is simply the ball spinning forward as it travels through the air, from the bottom over the top. Just the

opposite is under spin, where the ball is spinning backwards as it moves through the air. This spin will make the ball move through the air differently and spin in an opposite direction when it bounces. Topspin will have a tendency to jump forward and much higher as it bounces. Again, the opposite will be the case when hitting with backspin or underspin. The ball will slide or bite into the court as it bounces, causing it to stay much lower.

Always remember that tennis is a game for your lifetime. So wouldn't it make sense that your game has to evolve as you get older to maintain your level or maybe even improve your game?

Forehand

WHEN WATCHING PROFESSIONALS PLAY, WE SEE MANY WAYS TO HIT A FOREHAND - or any shot for that matter - but what we want to examine are the similarities in these shots.

○ *Early racquet preparation.*
○ *Lots of little steps setting up for the shot and big steps getting to the ball.*
○ *Keeping their weight back when their racquet is back.*
○ *Solid rotation of the core through the shot.*

This makes for a longer, faster swing giving you more power as well as more control. Don't try to over hit the ball. Be patient and your forehand will become a weapon.

There are plenty of options with the forehand. Some I recommend; others I don't. Let's take a look at some of them.

Let's start from the ground up. Where should you position your feet to maximize the stroke? This part of the stroke is often discussed and rarely agreed upon.

First, what I will call "old school" where we step in and across when the racquet is back. For anyone who hasn't played, this would be reaching to get to the ball with the opposite foot. This closed stance position leaves your weight in an uncomfortable position with your balance leaning forward. It causes the weight to shift in the wrong direction and almost guarantees the contact point to be very late - resulting in a poor shot which puts a lot of stress on the dominant arm. I discourage this stance for two reasons - first, the body cannot flow through the swing, which causes the arm to do the work, and second, the recovery step for the next shot will be much slower.

Another option would be the "square stance" where the feet are parallel to the side line of the court. With this stance, you are getting closer to finding the right position, as you

may have to be squarer in your stance when moving forward into the court, particularly when hitting an approach shot. Starting with the feet parallel to the sideline, you can initiate some hip rotation in the swing but it is still somewhat limited. Don't move your weight forward too soon. Keeping your weight back when the racquet is back helps maintain balance through the swing. By shifting forward too soon, your balance is tough to control and the ability to rotate your hips through the shot is limited. This second stance is an adequate option but still not preferred.

Another option is the "open stance" forehand. First, it is very important to remember that open stance does not mean you don't have to turn. Even with the stance more open, there is a big turn in the hips and shoulders. Initiate the swing by stepping out and slightly back with the right foot for right-handed players. Place the right foot parallel to the baseline. The left foot can be placed anywhere to the left of the plane of the right foot. As you can see, there is a lot of variation in this stance. It only makes sense to not be set in one exact spot on each shot. Not all balls hit to you are exactly the same. This is the stance or set up of choice on the forehand. It allows a quick set up, plenty of upper body rotation or coil and a recovery step that will amaze you and your opponents. The open-stance forehand is not just a stance for pros and top juniors. Older players can reap the benefits of being more open. Maybe not to the extent of Rafael Nadal but, like Nadal, you can certainly add power and control to your game.

The Backswing

As with the positioning of the feet during the forehand stroke, there are options on the backswing as well, straight back or a loop.

The loop backswing starts the backswing high, making a "C" motion. You can also bring the racquet straight back, just as it sounds, where the racquet goes directly back to a low position for the forward swing. Neither is wrong. You may even use both in different situations.

The straight-back backswing is exactly what it sounds like, when you turn to your back foot and rotate your shoulders the racquet goes straight back with the butt cap of the racquet pointing at the net. Your racquet arm relaxes and the racquet head is below your hand. With the loop backswing, the shoulder turn and takeaway happen together but the racquet is above your hand. As you initiate the swing, the racquet head drops or loops below your hand. Some players feel the timing is easier with the loop. It can be but I caution, you must start the swing earlier and keep the loop small in order to have enough time to have the proper contact point. The loop backswing is generally preferred by clay court players. If

you have a loop backswing, there is no need to change it but have the ability to modify the size of the loop, making it smaller when you are playing on a fast hard court or on a grass court.

When you start the backswing is also very important. The quicker you can read the ball coming off your opponents racquet, the easier it will be to have the contact point in the proper point in the swing.

Watch Venus and Serena Williams prepare for the shot, they have the quickest set up I have seen.

What to do with the opposite hand is more important than you may think. The old school thinking was to point at the ball as it is coming to you. My feeling is that you should rotate your shoulders in the preparation phase of the swing. This will bring the free hand around more ensuring a full shoulder turn. Feel as though your free hand is moving with your racquet hand. This will insure a full rotation with the shoulders. Your hands will feel as if you were holding a beach ball when you take the racquet back. This will also help to eliminate any crossing your hands on the follow which restricts the un-coiling of the shoulders with the forward swing of the racquet.

Contact Point and Follow Through

The forward swing to the ball begins with the right foot (right-handed players) pushing up and out off the court. This initiates the weight transfer and the rotation of the hips and shoulders through the stroke. The contact point of the swing varies depending on your grip. When hitting the continental grip forehand, the contact point is much later in the swing. As you move your grip around the handle of the racquet, the contact point is moved more forward and earlier in the swing. A forehand hit with a full western grip will have the contact point much more in front of the body. The push off from the back foot allows for a long faster swing, generating plenty of power. Keep the plane of the swing in a low to high path to increase the angle of the racquet at the point of impact, allowing you to hit more spin on a given shot. To increase the amount of topspin, close the racquet face in the backswing by turning the palm of your racquet hand down toward the court.

This changes the angle of the racquet face at the point of contact so with a full, fast follow through you are able to create extreme spin. A follow through over your opposite shoulder with your elbow pointing toward your target increases the rotation in your upper body and increases racquet head speed.

Remember to learn to hit the ball hard you must practice swinging the racquet faster. Try a ball machine. It won't complain if you don't hit the ball in the court. Exaggerate the racquet head speed as you swing through the ball. Without changing your equipment, the only way to hit the ball harder or faster is to swing the racquet faster. Try to think of swinging the racquet through the ball not hitting at the ball. This helps increase your racquet head speed.

Concentrate on swinging faster, not hitting harder. There is a difference.

Use the left hand to push the racquet back to help rotate the shoulders to the hitting position.

Following through on the forehand with the elbow pointing to the target will ensure a good rotation with the core.

Rotate the left shoulder as you swing the racquet to develop a full rotation with your entire body.

BACK TO BASICS:

○ Step first with the foot on the same side as the ball. Right-handed players step with the right foot and vice versa. By making this the first step, it ensures you are rotating the hips and shoulders in the backswing. Remember open stance does not mean you won't turn.

○ Your weight is on the back foot when the racquet is back. Be patient! This is a great tip to keep in mind when you are having trouble with those players who don't hit very hard, hold the weight back until you are ready to swing. It helps keep you in balance and keep the stroke under control.

○ Adjust the contact point to the type of grip. A western grip has an earlier contact point. This is essential in developing control and spin.

○ Rotate the hips and shoulders with the swing (avoid a big cross over step - it locks the hips and shortens the swing). This helps make the swing longer and faster resulting in more power.

○ Follow through with the elbow of your racquet arm pointing to your target. Where your elbow points does not help the flight of the ball. It is gone from your racquet by the time you follow through but it makes you rotate through the swing.

○ The back foot should finish on the toe; this insures the rotation of the hips and makes a stable base for the finish. Swing as hard or fast as you want as long as you stay in balance. Loss of balance certainly equals a loss of control.

○ The recovery step is very important. Once you have finished the swing, start the recovery by side stepping or shuffling toward the middle of the court. Remember to split step when your opponent starts to make their swing.

PRACTICE DRILL:

With your partner about 10 feet away and standing in a semi-open stance, throw a medicine ball, 6-8 pounds back and forth with both hands. Concentrate on rotating your shoulders when you catch the ball and un-coiling when you throw. Your back foot releases to your toe. Don't step through. This drill helps develop core strength and helps you develop the rotation needed in the forehand. Standing in the opposite direction for this drill is a great help for the two-handed backhand as well.

Backhand

THE BACKHAND HAS REMAINED A BIT MORE TRADITIONAL THAN THE NEW MORE OPEN stance forehand. That being said, let's try to make some adjustments in the backhand to make it more of a strength on the court. No longer will our opponents say "just hit to his/her backhand and you'll win the point." Our goal is to be equally strong off both sides.

The forehand and two-handed backhand are based on rotational swings with the dominant arm swinging across our body. We need the rotation of our hips and shoulders to clear our body from the path of the swing and allow the racquet to accelerate through the ball. The one-handed backhand is much more of a linear swing, with your arm swinging

away from your body. Here, keep our body much more sideways and balanced to accelerate the racquet through the contact point of the swing.

One-handed Backhand

Hitting the backhand with one hand is a little less stable than the two-handed backhand but with the proper footwork, grip and timing this can be a very graceful and effective shot with a lot of variety. We can drop the racquet head and close the face to hit with a great deal of topspin or we can start the racquet head higher and more open to hit through the ball with underspin or slice. Slice, topspin or flat backhands are similar in body movement. The difference is the starting position of the racquet, the plane of the swing through the ball and the follow through.

If you are trying to develop a topspin or slice backhand, it is very important that you keep your body sideways through the swing. If your shoulders open on the swing, the racquet face will also open at contact and the ball will tend to go high and long. Staying sideways through the shot helps keep the racquet head moving through the plane of the ball.

PRACTICE DRILL:

Standing sideways with a ball in your racquet hand, hold the ball next to your left hip, for right-handed players, and simply throw the ball across the net to the back fence with a backhand motion. Keeping your shoulders sideways and releasing the wrist on the throw will give you a great feel for the one-handed backhand. This will give you the feel of a full follow through on the one-handed backhand. This drill can also give you a feel of how to direct the ball from one side of the court to the other. With the same motion throw a few balls cross court and then down the line. This is exactly the feel you will need to direct the ball on your backhand.

BACK TO BASICS:

○ Step first with the foot on the same side as the ball (the left foot for right-handed players). This turns your hips and shoulders while preparing you to move to the ball. At this point, the racquet should be prepared (take the racquet back) for the shot.

○ Weight is back when the racquet is back. Try to hold your weight on the back foot until the swing starts forward, transferring the weight as the racquet moves through the contact point of the stroke.

○ In the backswing, close the racquet face to hit with topspin, or open it to hit with underspin. This can be done by rolling the knuckles toward the court for topspin and to the sky for slice. Dropping the racquet head much lower, below the contact point of the swing, allows you to generate a great deal of topspin. Use your free hand to pull the racquet back. This helps you control the angle of the backswing and generate the desired spin on the shot.

○ Step into the court with the right foot (right-handed players), not across your body. By having the weight transferring in the direction of the shot, it allows you to swing faster through the ball, thus generating a much stronger shot.

○ Contact with the ball is slightly in front of the right foot. The more closed and down the racquet head is in the backswing, the more the contact point has to be front of the body. If the racquet face is slightly open and underspin is the goal, the contact point is much closer to the body.

○ As you start the racquet forward, pull your free hand back (much like an umpire making a safe sign) to keep your shoulders sideways to the net. This simple move helps keep the racquet head moving through the contact point and allows you to follow through the plane of the ball to get the desired depth and spin.

○ For topspin, finish high and in front. Release the wrist on the follow through like throwing a frisbee. The release of the wrist adds racquet head speed, which increases power through the full swing.

○ When hitting the ball with underspin or slice, avoid chopping at the ball. This swing feels as if you are sliding the ball off a table top with a very smooth motion through the ball. The wrist rolls under the contact point allowing the racquet to impart underspin. The racquet finishes up and slightly open on the follow through.

○ Recover back to the athletic ready position anticipating the move to the next shot.

The backswing on the one-handed backhand can take on a lot of variations. Make sure to prepare early and drop the racquet below the level of the ball to hit a topspin shot. Some of the top players will take the racquet back high and drop the racquet head before swinging forward.

The slice backhand can be a very effective tool in your game. Use a higher backswing and a slightly open racquet face. Remember to hit through the ball, it is not a chopping motion.

Two-handed Backhand

The biggest difference between the one-handed and two-handed backhand, besides the obvious second hand on the racquet, is how much your body moves through the swing. As we discussed earlier, the one-handed backhand is a linear swing with the hips and shoulders remaining somewhat sideways through the entire swing. The two-handed backhand requires the body to rotate through the swing as if you are hitting a left-handed forehand for right-handed players.

As with the one-handed backhand, we initiate the swing by turning the left foot parallel to the baseline and placing it slightly behind the right foot. This move rotates the hips and shoulders preparing the racquet for the stroke. Keeping your hands close to your left hip (for right-handed players) sets you up to take a rip at the backhand. Remember, this is a left-hand dominate swing that feels as if you are driving the racquet through the ball. The weight transfers from your left foot to your right by pushing off from the left foot, rotating your hips and shoulders as you accelerate the racquet through the contact point of the swing. Finish over your right shoulder with the elbows high. Imagine you are wearing a watch on your left arm; now finish with your watch next to your right ear.

Since this shot is very similar in structure to a forehand, work the rotation of the hips. Direction can be gained by pointing the left elbow to the desired target (right-handed players). By the time you point your elbow to the target, the ball is long off your strings. This thinking does help with developing the proper rotation on the swing. Stay relaxed and allow the body to flow with the swing.

If you hit a two-handed backhand, topspin is your shot of choice. But to hit with slice, use one hand or, at least, release the left hand as you swing forward. It is important to keep the shoulders sideways to the net to avoid the racquet face opening on contact.

BACK TO BASICS:

○ Preparation is similar to that of the one-handed backhand. Always step first with the foot on the side that the ball is coming from. Turn your left foot and step to the side to prepare for the two-handed backhand for right-handed players.

○ Keep the weight back when the racquet is back. Holding your weight on the back foot longer allows the transfer of weight as the racquet is moving through the contact point of the swing. This helps keep everything in balance as you swing. The "old school" thinking of step in and get your racquet back just doesn't work.

○ In the backswing, start with your hands close to your left pocket for right-handed players. This gives you a solid reference point to start the swing. For high or very low balls, there will be some adjusting to this starting point but it is a great place to start when developing a new two-handed backhand.

○ For right-handed players, use your left hand. This shot is very similar to hitting a left-handed forehand. If the right hand becomes dominate, the swing will be a pull rather than a drive resulting in a weaker grip and, consequently, a much weaker shot.

○ Avoid a big cross-over step as it locks your hips and limits the swing. Rotate your hips and shoulders, eliminating a lot of the pressure off your lower back. The rotation makes the swing longer, resulting in a faster, more powerful stroke.

○ Follow through over your right shoulder for right-handed players, as if you were listening to your watch on your left wrist with your right ear. This little trick will guarantee a solid follow through and help keep the racquet on a low-to-high path resulting in more topspin.

○ Finish with the back foot on the toe, which assures you have rotated your hips and works as a balance point. This looks a little like the finish of a golf swing, but don't hold the position very long; just long enough to finish the shot and maintain your balance.

○ Recover back to your athletic ready position.

82

Approach Shots

WHAT IS AN APPROACH SHOT?

In the most basic sense, an approach is any shot that you come into the court on, i.e. approach the net. That being said, there are a lot of variables as to where, when and how to hit an effective approach shot. Your personal style of play will have a great effect on what an approach shot is and how you use it in your game. How aggressive do you want to play? Do you enjoy playing at the net or are you a baseline player who only comes to the net to shake hands? Keeping all of our options in mind, let's take a look at some of the keys to hitting an effective approach shot.

When moving forward to hit an approach shot, you will need to make some adjustments in your swing to avoid over hitting the shot. As you are moving to the ball, turn your front shoulder toward the net – right shoulder for the backhand and left shoulder for the forehand for right-handed players. When hitting an underspin approach shot, shorten your backswing. A good rule of thumb to follow is the closer you get to the net, the shorter your backswing needs to be. Follow through; avoid hitting and stopping your swing. Stopping your swing short will result in a loss of control of the shot. If you are looking to hit the approach shot with topspin, close the face of the racquet slightly by turning the hitting face toward the court. This changes the angle of the racquet at the point of contact resulting in more spin and more control.

Most players come to the net if their opponent hits a ball that brings them inside the baseline for their next shot, somewhere in no-mans land. You hit the shot somewhere between the baseline and the service line. Some players are more aggressive on which balls they come in on, others more passive, retreating back behind the baseline. Deciding when to come in is a personal choice, a lot of which depends on your personal style of play.

When moving inside the baseline, it is best to hit the majority of your approach shots down the line. This shot makes covering the angles on the court much easier. When hitting from no-man's land, make your shot and move in closer to the net, following the ball that you hit. This will position yourself in the middle of your opponent's possible angles of return. Although most of the approach shots go down the line, avoid hitting all of your approach shots to the same side of the court. Mix it up; if you always go down the line, your opponent may start to move to that side of the court and have a much easier passing shot. Remember, a cross court approach shot opens up the court and you will have to move farther to cover the possible angles of return. It is, however, an effective shot if you have time to swing out, looking to hit a winner.

The three most important aspects of an effective approach shot.

Depth is Best: By hitting the approach shot deep, it allows you more time to get into the net. It also gives you more time to react to your opponents return and open up the short angle volley to win the point.

Direction is Second: Choose the direction of the shot to make covering the court easier or to exploit an obvious weakness in your opponents' game. Don't be anxious about attacking either your opponent's forehand or backhand if they have an apparent weakness.

Pace (Speed) is Third: Try to be purposeful and assertive with your approach shots. Do not try to over power your opponent to win the point. Give your opponent a chance to miss. This is a set up shot, get to the net and win the point with the volley.

Spins

Conventional thinking tells us to always hit our approach shot with underspin. Underspin will keep the ball low and will force your opponent to hit up. This will allow you to hit the volley from above the net, making it an easier put-away shot for you.

In today's big topspin game, an approach shot with topspin will drive your opponent back, forcing them into hitting a defensive shot. If topspin is your normal shot, by all means use it for your approach shots as well. Don't re-invent the wheel. Keep it simple. Both shots hit well can be very effective.

So when deciding if topspin or slice is a better choice, your best bet will always be to choose the option you hit the most often. If you hit topspin from the baseline, that would be an effective choice for your approach shot. However, if you are chasing a short ball, a controlled slice may be a better option. Experiment with all types of shots and keep learning. That's what keeps all of this so much fun.

When approaching the net, ALWAYS make a solid split step or check step, (more on that later), as your opponent makes contact with his/her shot. This keeps you balanced through the shot and makes it much easier to react to the return.

Even if you are a die hard baseliner, make yourself come to the net on short balls. It adds a new dimension to your game and makes the game a lot more fun.

A word of caution. When you do decide to come in to the net, your opponent may hit a lob. Don't be over concerned with this happening until they prove they can hit an effective lob. A great way to defend against the lob is to develop a strong overhead. Be aggressive and don't worry about a few lost points. Nothing will work every time. The game would be pretty boring if it did.

The Split Step

The split step isn't something only for the best players. All players must make this an essential part of their game. You may not always get inside the service line after your approach shot. How hard, high and deep you hit the ball are determining factors as to when you will make the split step.

Split step when your opponent starts their swing. A split step or check step readies you for your opponent's shot. In other words, when the ball moves away from you, move forward. When the ball stops moving, make your split step. It will also make changing direction to get to the next shot much easier.

The split step gets your feet under your body for a more balanced feeling to adjust to the next ball. It should not be a jump stop. It is only to get balanced and move to the next shot.

By following the approach shot to the net and making the split step, you are much more under control and it will be easier to make the first volley. By no means if you hit the first volley from the service line is your job finished. Follow the ball to cover your opponent's possible angles of return, making another split step when your opponent is making their next swing.

The First Volley

In addition to following the ball, close into the net as your shot goes away from you. This cuts down the angles your opponent has to pass you and will also open the court for better angles on your second volley. The best volley position is about half way between the net and service line.

As you aggressively move toward the net, don't get too close. When you get so close to the net you can touch it, you will become much more susceptible to the lob.

Cutting off the Angles

Don't think you have to win the point on the first ball; be prepared to move in, split step and put the ball away on the second volley. It is much easier to hit two good shots to the win the point rather one great, low percentage shot.

Specialty Shots

THESE SHOTS ALL REQUIRE A GREAT DEAL OF PRACTICE TO DEVELOP TOUCH OR FEEL to hit successfully. They won't be used often but are great shots to have in your repertoire because they are fun to hit and even more fun to watch your opponent chase down. The element of surprise is very important when using any of these shots.

Knowing not only how to hit these specialty shots is important but knowing when to attempt them is equally important. Try not to overuse any of them. We don't want our opponent to know when they are coming.

The Drop Shot

Just as it sounds, you are trying to drop the ball just over the net with as little pace as possible. The drop shot should be attempted when your opponent is behind the baseline and you are inside your baseline. If you attempt a drop shot from behind your baseline the ball has to travel much too far to get to the net, giving your opponent plenty of time to run it down. Disguise is another important aspect of any touch shot, especially the drop shot. The later your opponent recognizes you are hitting short, the less time there is for them to react to your shot.

When hitting a drop shot, the backswing should look very similar to any other groundstroke but just before you make contact, soften or loosen your grip and roll the racquet face under the ball with an abbreviated follow through.

The best grip to use when hitting an effective drop shot is the continental grip, as it allows you to roll the wrist under the ball. This takes the speed off of your shot, essentially dropping the ball over the net.

Since you are hitting this ball from inside the baseline, follow your shot into the net. In

the event that your opponent does get to your drop shot, you will be in the best position to cover all the possible angles of return.

Never celebrate your great shot until you know the point is over. Many times I've seen players make a good drop shot and stop playing, thinking they have won the point. The opponent gets to the ball and wins the point just by getting the ball back in play.

If you are playing a true baseline player, the drop shot effectively brings your opponent out of their element. Hitting even a marginal drop shot forces your opponent to come to the net where they may not feel as comfortable.

When you have hit a good drop shot, move in toward the ball. If your opponent is on the dead run, the chance of them hitting a great shot is pretty slim. By moving in, you put added pressure on them as they run to get to your drop shot.

Lobs

The lob can be hit in two different but equally effective ways, offensive to win the point or defensive to keep you in the point. Let's look at both of them.

But first, as with all touch or feel shots, the element of surprise is very important. Try to make the backswing in each of these shots look just like a groundstroke. Either offensive or defensive the lob can be quite effective and frustrating for your opponent.

Defensive Lobs

The best grip for hitting this shot is the same grip you use when hitting a normal ground-stroke. By keeping the grip you are comfortable with, you can hit the lob with the most confidence. Usually this shot is used when you are out of position and you need time to get back in the court and ready for the next shot. That being said, you may not always have the time you need to set up and make the shot exactly as you would like. Try to keep your weight back when your racquet is back, similar to any groundstroke. The backswing is also very similar, probably a little lower to allow you to get the right amount of lift on the shot. At contact, the racquet face is slightly open and still somewhat in front of your body. A long high, full finish that is slightly higher than usual will give you the depth you need on the shot. Any slowing or stopping of the follow through results in a short lob and big problems for you when your opponent is hitting overheads back at you.

More often than not, the defensive lob is hit too short rather than too long. When you are practicing, make sure you are working on getting the feel for the depth and height of each lob. This takes some practice but it is a pretty easy touch shot to master. To help de-

velop touch on your lobs, have the peak of the trajectory be over the net. If the trajectory peaks too early, the ball will land short in the court and, conversely, if the ball peaks late, it will probably land out of the court.

This shot can be used successfully when you are pulled way out of position or are running down a tough shot by your opponent. It is great to use when you need a little more time to make your shot and get back in the point.

Offensive Lobs

Sometimes called the attacking lob, the offensive lob is hit to win the point not just to get back in the point. It is a little lower in trajectory and with much more topspin. The effectiveness of this shot relies on disguise. The set up and backswing look identical to the set up for any open stance topspin groundstroke. As we have discussed, when the racquet goes back, the weight goes back with a full rotation of the hips and shoulders. The racquet should be turned slightly more closed with the hitting face toward the ground. This set up allows you to hit with the most topspin. The contact point is very early with the racquet, moving up as you come through the ball. The follow through will be high, with a feeling of brushing up the back of the ball. Make sure you use a full rotation of the hips and shoulders to ensure a full swing through the ball. The trajectory of this shot isn't quite as high as the defensive lob and the spin makes it jump away from your opponent when it bounces.

Don't over think this shot. Look at it as a very high topspin groundstroke. It is very effective from both the forehand and backhand side. When developing this shot, practice by varying the height of your normal groundstrokes, some lower, some higher, some really high and, *voila* – you are hitting a topspin lob. It's not magic but you do need a reasonable amount of practice. Try to use this shot when your opponent is coming into the net and you have little time to get set to make the shot.

With either lob, if your opponent moves back in the court and lets the ball drop, move in. When they move back, you move in, making the transition from defense to offense.

Cross Court Roller

Another one of my favorite touch shots is the cross court roller. You hit this shot with either the forehand or backhand when your opponent is coming to the net. Simply set up to hit a traditional groundstroke with the backswing slightly more closed, hit the ball very early and roll the racquet face over the ball. Make it drop on the side "T" of the service box.

All of these shots can be a lot of fun and add a considerable amount of variety to your game. Keep in mind you may never master all the shots but its great fun to try.

Serve

THE SERVE HAS BEEN CALLED THE MOST IMPORTANT SHOT IN THE GAME. EVERY point does in fact start with someone serving. With that said, I do believe the serve is the most important shot but it is also the most difficult to master. With both hands moving in opposite directions, we need to coordinate a lot of different movements to orchestrate a successful serve. With a few tricks and a lot of practice you can develop a very effective serve.

There are as many styles of serves as there are tennis players. As a matter of fact, no two players serve exactly alike. That being said, all good servers do have a lot in common. As we look at the service motion I will break down its important elements, remembering there will be a lot of ways to get the job done.

Important to Remember

The serve is the only shot in the game that you get to hit when you want to hit it! All of the other shots you have to hit when the ball is in the right place, or in other words, when it gets to you.

When learning to serve, start slowly, break the stroke down to its parts. Allowing your body to move forward as you toss will make it easier to control the height and placement of the toss. Try not to just throw the ball up and chase it by changing your swing. This will result in an ineffective service motion. Simply said, keep the swing the same and place your toss in the path of the racquet.

Serving is a lot of fun and if done well can create some free points. Experiment with some new things and develop different types of serves, slice, flat even a topspin serve.

All good servers will move forward on the serve. Keeping the fingers of the toss hand pointing to the net will help keep the toss forward, allowing you to move into the court on the serve. Roger Federer (left) jumps up and forward during his serve, allowing him to swing faster. This will increase the racquet head speed on the serve and add pace to the serve.

Keeping the service motion relaxed from the start will help increase racquet head speed and power on your serve. Tight muscles will be slow. Relaxed muscles will be much faster. Racquet head speed on the serve is how you will increase the speed of your serve.

LET'S BREAK IT DOWN:

○ First and foremost, relax. You won't be able to do much with your serve if you are holding your breath and if you have a death grip on the handle of your racquet.

○ Start with a comfortable stance. Your front foot should ideally be about a 45-degree angle to the baseline and with the back foot shoulder width from the front foot and parallel to the baseline. Line your feet up to your target, once your feet are set, draw an imaginary line from one toe to the other. It should point directly at the service box you are trying to hit.

○ Start with your weight on the back foot and shift your weight forward with the lift of your toss hand.

○ When beginning the placement of the ball (the toss), start by holding the ball in the fingertips of your non-dominate hand. Also, only hold one ball at a time. It is easier to control the toss. I have always thought holding two balls is a bit pessimistic. Slowly lift, placing the ball in position while you keep your finger-tips pointing to the net. If your fingertips point to the sky when making the toss, the ball may go back over your head.

○ As you make the toss, your weight moves forward with the left hip pushing forward as the toss hand comes up for right-handed players. You will have the nice top of a trophy pose when you release the ball. If you are moving backward, the ball is certain to be too far behind you.

○ Conventional wisdom says that we need to throw the ball as high as possible to have more time to hit the serve. In reality, we do not need more time to hit the serve, just the right amount of time. Toss only as high as you can reach with your racquet, making the swing without any hitch or hesitation in the motion. A lower toss promotes a smooth swing; without stopping or slowing to wait for the ball to fall into your strike zone.

○ In the backswing portion of the motion, the butt cap of the racquet points to the sky. This allows plenty of racquet head acceleration up and through the contact point. Keep your grip very loose. If you are tight with the grip you definitely will be slow with the swing.

○ Feel the wrist snap or break at the point of contact, similar to throwing a ball. This will help increase racquet head speed allowing you to hit the ball with more speed/pace.

○ After full extension to the contact point and plenty of acceleration through the ball, follow through to the opposite side of your body. Allow your back foot to move into the court completing the swing. Some players will jump off their front foot landing on the same foot, the similarity here is both are movements forward into the court.

Flat Serve

The flat serve is usually used as a first serve. This serve is hit with the least amount of spin giving the ball more speed or pace but also greatly reducing your margin of error. The grip of choice is the continental grip. Toss the ball further in front of your body, more into the court, to allow the racquet head to move forward through the ball. Keep your arm and wrist very relaxed, much like throwing a baseball, giving you the most racquet head speed for more power. When you finish this swing, you are well inside the baseline. Don't be reluctant to really move through and into this serve. At first, this serve may feel a bit out of control but keep moving in, use your legs and swing fast. Have fun!

Slice or Spin Serve

Adjust your grip slightly to the backhand position and toss the ball slightly more to the right for a slice/spin serve. This will allow you to automatically hit the ball with a lot of spin. The toss on the spin/slice serve will be closer to you, not as far into the court as the flat serve. Your first few attempts may send the ball from right to left and probably into the net (for right-handed players). While learning, forget about where the ball is going and get used to the grip and the spin. Make adjustments to your target area as you become more accustomed to the grip change. Pick a target much higher over the net and much more to the right. Let the ball spin itself back into the court. Avoid trying to steer or baby the spin serve into the court. Always swing through the contact point. Swing through the ball with plenty of racquet head speed and snap or release the wrist. The angle of the racquet will add the spin you need and keep the ball in the court.

Topspin

For topspin, adjust your grip toward the backhand position like the slice serve. Toss the ball more over your head, slightly over your front shoulder to allow the upward movement of the swing. You may need to arch your back and relax your wrist. Aim higher over the net and keep practicing. To develop the desired spin, use a lot of wrist hitting up and snapping the wrist up and out. Try standing very still with your feet and body and hitting up and through with just your wrist as you get some feel on the arc of the swing. Then slowly start to incorporate your legs into the motion of the serve as you practice. This is the most difficult serve to master and the hardest on your body. Be careful and practice smart.

Remember you always sacrifice speed for spin and spin for speed!

Checking yourself: If your serves go consistently long, your toss is probably too far be-hind your head. On the other hand, if you miss into the net, you may be dropping your toss hand too quickly. This will make you drop your head and you will hit a lot of balls into the net. This will also help your extension up and through the contact point of the serve. As you practice the various serves, hit a few flat serves, then hit some spin serves and hit some flat serves again. Don't just practice one type of serve. Mix it up; make it similar to playing in a match. It becomes similar to a pitcher in baseball who only throws fastballs. Eventually the hitters will figure out how to hit the pitch. The most effective pitchers have a lot of variety; curve balls, fast balls and change ups. We should approach our service games the same way. Keep'em guessing and mix it up.

PRACTICE TIP:

My old friend, Townsend Gilbert, showed me a great practice exercise for the serve. Simply tie an old sneaker to the end of your racquet and try your service motion, without hitting a ball. The weight of the shoe makes your backswing fuller, forcing you to extend to the full height of the swing. This forces you to follow through to the proper side of your body.

Return of Serve

IF THE SERVE IS THE MOST IMPORTANT SHOT IN THE GAME IT MAKES SENSE THAT THE return of serve is the second most important shot in the game. Some of the best players in the world have had adequate serves but developed unbelievable return games that lifted them to the top. Jimmy Connors and Andre Agassi are arguably the best returners the game has ever seen.

"Keep it simple" holds true for the entire game but it is even more important with the return of serve. There is very little time to make this shot, so any extra movement will only make it more difficult.

Let's get started...

○ Start a step or two deeper than normal. As your opponent is making the toss for the serve, move forward with shuffle or hop step. When the server makes contact with the ball, split step and be ready to move to either side for the return. Your starting position varies, sometimes greatly, depending on the strength of your opponents serve. When returning a second serve, move forward a step or two into the court. Unless you are playing Pete Sampras on a regular basis, almost no one has a second serve that is as effective as the first.

○ Focus on the ball. This sounds obvious but most of the time we focus on the ball too late, making contact late and causing our shot to be out of control. Try to follow your opponents toss hand up. Focus on the ball from the moment they release the toss. Begin your movement at that precise instant.

○ Try to read the toss and the service motion. If you pay attention, most players move the ball or their body when they serve to different corners of the court or with different

spins. Be aware of things your opponent may adjust and look for that serve.

○ Shorten your backswing. Though easier said than done, with some practice it works. The faster the serve, the less time you have to swing so it makes sense that a shorter swing makes the contact point easier to dial in.

○ Accelerate through the ball. Though you shorten the backswing, by no means do you shorten your follow through. Avoid slowing the racquet down through the contact point. Accelerate through the ball.

○ Follow through. On an offensive return, the follow will be long, similar to a full ground-stroke. Hit out, going for speed and spin. On a defensive return, shorten the follow through to match the backswing - almost like a volley resulting in what will feel like a blocking motion that results in slice or chip type return.

By making the move forward, you are able to stay on the balls of your feet, allowing you to be more aggressive on the return. Don't be afraid to hit through a second serve and move into the net. Your aggressive return on a weaker second serve will tactically put you in charge of the point. This will work in both singles and doubles.

With some practice you will find a swing and position on the court that best fits your style of play. Experiment with different positions on the court and altering the length of your follow through. You may even move a little more right or left if your opponent seems to have a stronger serve to one side or the other. A great thing to remember is you don't have to hit all of your returns hard. Try some fun shots off the return. When playing doubles and your opponents are trying to serve and volley on every point, try a lob over the net players head. If they are staying back, try a short ball hit short cross court and come in to the net. There are endless options. Keep having fun and experiment with all of the return variations.

Court Anatomy

WHEN PLAYING TENNIS, THE THINGS YOU SHOULD AND SHOULD NOT TRY ARE OFTEN dictated by your position on the court. There are three areas of the court to be familiar with: the baseline or back court area; "no-mans land" or the middle of the court between the baseline and the service line, also called the approach zone; and the put-away area, or the net where volleys are easy winners. Let's call it, grind, attack and finish. In all of these areas of the court, there are distinct skills necessary to be successful, from hitting groundstrokes in the backcourt to sticking your volleys at the net. Learn to play the entire court. We have already discussed these skills; now let's define the specific areas of the court.

The Baseline Area

From the area of the court behind the baseline, you can control the pace and depth of the ball with your groundstrokes. Develop the mindset of a grinder. You will begin to recognize that some groundstrokes will be hit defensively while others must be hit with an offensive mindset. By moving your opponent from side to side and bringing them to the net, you draw errors or make them hit weak shots that you can turn into winners. From this part of the court you will try to maneuver your opponent to an area of the court where you can win the point or force a short ball that you can attack. Patience is the key when playing from the baseline. Plenty of net clearance and depth on your shots keep your opponent back and gives you a clear advantage. Your patterns of play are important. We will discuss a bit more on that later.

No-Mans Land

Try to develop the mentality of an attacking player when you get the ball that lands shorter in the court. I am sure you have heard, "Don't play from no-mans land," but the fact is you have to hit shots from the middle area of the court. The ball is going to land in no-mans land and, unless you want to hand the point to your opponent, you have to hit it from there. The key is to hit the ball and move either up to the net or retreat back to the baseline. Attack or grind, this is where you have to make a choice. Do not stand and wait for the next ball. Your decision on which direction to go depends a great deal on where you prefer to play. If your preference is either the net or the baseline, make a choice and move. Developing your net game may make the choice easier. Having the option of coming to the net or staying back makes you a much better player and gives you a well-rounded game. By staying in the middle of the court, you are making your life much tougher than it needs to be. Any ball hit deep will force you to hit a volley or balls hit mid court will result in the need to hit a half volley. Either way, it is much tougher than moving in to the net or back to the baseline.

The Net Area

At the net area, your driving thought is to finish the point. Playing the net will become a lot of fun. Force your opponent to move around, creating an open area in the court where you can put the ball away with an easy volley. Moving forward opens up angles that you may have never thought of hitting. By moving in towards the net, you force your opponent to react much faster while positioning yourself for the possible angles of their return. You can look like an all-star. What about the lob? Don't anticipate the lob until your opponent can prove they can hit it consistently. All the time I see players backing up, opening up the angles and saying "I'm covering the lob" even though their opponents have not lobbed the entire match. Keep the pressure on. Keep moving in until they prove they can beat you with a lob.

Remember: Grind-Attack-Finish

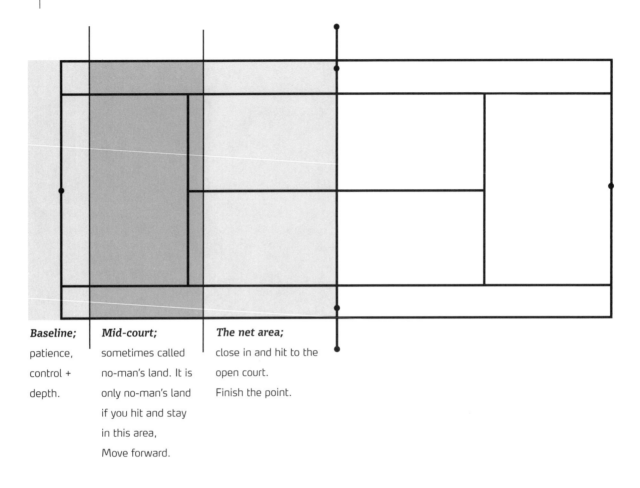

Baseline;

patience,
control +
depth.

Mid-court;

sometimes called
no-man's land. It is
only no-man's land
if you hit and stay
in this area,
Move forward.

The net area;

close in and hit to the
open court.
Finish the point.

Where the areas of the court start and stop is definitely a gray area. You have to decide where no-mans land starts and stops for your game. It varies for each player and depends on your individual style of play. When you play doubles, I strongly recommend that you push yourself to get to net. Moving forward cuts off your opponents angles and opens up the court for your return. Playing side by side rather than one up and one back makes you a stronger doubles team: but more on that later. We all have strengths and weaknesses on the tennis court, so work on the weak areas of your game and continue developing your strengths.

Dissecting the Court

Now that you have an understanding of the areas of the court, learning to play in each area is much easier. Simple adjustments to your game in these different areas make controlling the point much easier.

The Back Court/Baseline

The back court, or baseline area of the court, is sometimes called the "maneuvering zone." Quite simply, it is the part of the court that requires patience to develop the point. In a cross court rally, to keep the ball going cross court is simpler than to change the direction of the ball. The cross court return is a higher percentage play because the court is longer and the net is a lower. It is always easier to continue hitting the ball in the same direction than it is changing the direction. Cross court to cross court is easier than cross court to down the line. When in doubt, hit the groundstroke cross court with a little more height. This buys you some time to get into position for the next shot, hopefully a shot you have more time to set up and hit with an aggressive shot. If your opponent has an obvious weakness, by all means attack that side. Keep it simple. Be very patient when playing from this part of the court.

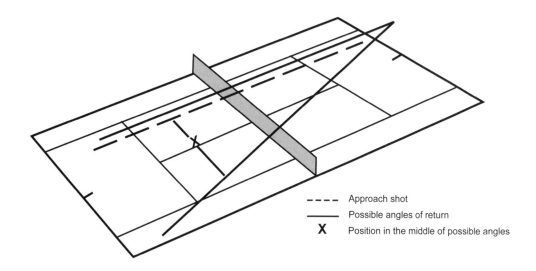

```
- - - -   Approach shot
_____   Possible angles of return
   X      Position in the middle of possible angles
```

The Middle or No-Man's Land

When your opponent returns a ball that lands short in your court, move forward turning your non-dominant shoulder toward the ball while shortening your backswing for a more controlled swing. Drive through the ball with either topspin or slice as we discussed earlier. Remember this is only "no-man's land" if you hit the ball and stand there. The key to an effective approach shot is depth. By keeping your shot deep, it gives you more time to get to the net and more time to react to your opponent's shot. This is not designed to be a "winner" but a set-up shot that allows you to get to the net and put the ball away. If your opponent's shot is slightly deeper, you may want to move and hit the shot and return to the area behind the baseline. There is no need to force the action. There are plenty of short balls you can feel comfortable coming in on.

The Net

Playing at the net can be a bit intimidating. It doesn't have to be. Just think about a couple of simple tips to make it a lot of fun.

1. Follow your approach shot forward, moving with the ball. Or look at it as shadowing your opponent. This allows you to cover the highest percentage angles of your opponent's return.
2. Eliminate your backswing and place the shot away from your opponent.
3. Keep moving until your opponent is about to hit their shot, then make your split step. It may take two volleys to win the point, so don't over hit.

Developing the Point

From the backcourt, patience is the key. Moving the ball from side to side and changing pace and spin will add to your success. If you get a short, off-speed ball, look to come in to the net. Remember, the closer you get to the net, the shorter your backswing. After you hit the approach shot, follow the ball that you hit or if you hit down the line, cover down the line. If you go crosscourt, cover crosscourt. When you go to the net, the service line is not close enough, you may have to volley from the service line but use that shot as another approach shot and continue to follow the ball you have hit and move further in.

Court Geometry

Geometry: a branch of mathematics that deals with measurement, properties and relationships of point, lines and angles.
- Merriam-Webster Dictionary

Geometry plays an extremely important part in your success or failure on the tennis court. Understanding the angles and distance in each possible play helps you cover the court more effectively as well as being able to move your opponent out of position.

The Best Volley Position

The best volley position is about half way between the service line and the net. This allows you to move forward as you hit your volley and still cover most of the attempted lobs. Don't park yourself there. It is only a starting position. Movement is vital.

This position cuts down the angles your opponent has available and allows you to better cover the court. As you move in to the net, the angles that you are able to hit open up the court to win the point.

The closer you get to the net, the more angles are cut down. Be careful, don't overdo it. Getting too close does not allow much reaction time either for the volley or to reach a lob.

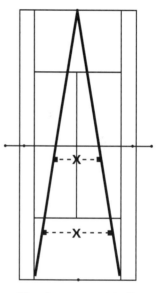

The closer you get to the net, the less distance there is between the possible angles of return.

Lateral Movement

Position yourself between all of your opponent's possible angles of return. Don't always recover to the center. Recover to the point on the court that allows you to best cover the potential shots your opponent may hit.

This shows the potential returns aren't always best covered by being in the center of the court or the center of your half of the court in doubles.

This means you move slightly side to side as well as forward to achieve the best volley position. Move with each shot. It will allow you to take away the high percentage shot and give your opponent the lower percentage short cross court ball.

Approach Shots

Though covered, earlier approach shots bear repeating.

Deeper is best: By keeping the approach deep, you have more time to get to the net and react to your opponent's return.

Direction is second: Choose the direction of the shot that makes covering the court easier or exploits an obvious weakness in your opponent's game.

Pace is third: Don't try to win the point on the approach shot. Give your opponent a chance to miss. Set up your next shot for a winner. Get to the net to win the point with a volley.

When approaching the net, ALWAYS make your split step as your opponent starts his/her swing. This makes it much easier to react to the return.

Dissect the Court

You don't always have to recover to the middle of the court. When playing from the baseline, try dissecting the court through the center "T" of the court to your opponent. In other words, draw an imaginary line from your opponent through the center "T" of the court on your side and that is where you should line up. As your opponent moves from side to side, move your imaginary line and move with your opponent.

When returning serve, move with the server. As he moves out toward the sideline you can move a step to the opposite side line. If your opponent is serving from the sideline, it is difficult for them to serve down the middle.

Trajectory

The trajectory, or arc of the ball over the net, should be at its highest point when the ball is crossing the net. If the height of your shot is on the far side of the court, the ball has a good chance of going long. Conversely, if the arc or height of your shot is on your side of the court, the ball may go in the net or land short in your opponent's side of the court putting you on the defensive.

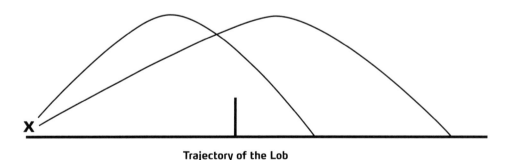

Trajectory of the Lob

If the height of the shot is before the net, the Lob will fall short.
Hit the Lob to peak on the opposite side of the net.

CHAPTER 21

Developing A Style of Play

IT HAS BEEN SAID AND OFTEN WRITTEN THAT OUR TRUE PERSONALITY SHOWS ON THE tennis court. This is certainly true. A person with a more laid back personality opts to play a more patient baseline game, while the player with a more aggressive personality leans a bit more toward a serve and volley style of play. Let's take a look at styles of play and how they best fit your personality. There are a lot of ways to play this great game, so find your most productive style.

The Baseline Player

The baseline player tends to be more patient with a fairly steady personality. Often called a "backboard" or "counter puncher," this player is usually quick-footed and willing to run down almost any ball. They win matches by not making mistakes. They keep the ball in play and make you lose the point. They are incredibly patient and are willing to stay on the court for as long as it takes.

The most effective way to play a baseline player is to make them do the thing they don't like to do: come to the net. Hit short balls and make them come in where they are uncomfortable. Another tactic is being more aggressive by coming to the net more and forcing the pace of the game. This takes away the angles and makes the baseliner become a shot maker.

The Serve and Volley Player

The serve and volleyer plays the most aggressively. This player prefers to come to the net on every opportunity, never letting the point carry on more than two or three shots. They always get to the net where they use their attacking skills with good approach shots, solid volleys and a strong overhead. The serve and volleyer usually plays as well as they serve. If the first serve isn't working, it could be a long difficult day for them.

The most effective way to play against a serve and volley player is to keep the ball deep. When they do come in, hit your return at their feet or hit wide to either side. This is a great way to slow them down. Changing the pace of the ball is also very effective against an aggressive serve and volley player. They usually don't move as well side to side, so keep your groundstrokes deep and move the ball around. The lob is also effective.

The All-Court Player

The all-court player may be the most difficult to play. They do everything pretty well and are somewhat comfortable all over the court. Look for weaknesses or strengths when playing this type of player. Usually they have a preference of staying back or coming to net. Exploit what they don't like to do. Analyzing their preference is a key to defeating the all-court player. You may have to vary your game. Change the pace of the game. Hit the ball side to side and short and make them move around the court looking for their weaknesses.

To become an all-court player, start by analyzing what kind of player you are now. Then work to develop the skills that you lack. Possibly your weakness is your footwork or your volleys, so spend some time working on these weaknesses. But don't forget to keep developing your strengths. If you are fortunate enough to have a coach, work with them to develop your style and keep working to develop an all-court game. Develop the areas of your game that aren't quite to the standard you have set.

Strategy

Strategy, A: a careful plan or method, B: the art of devising or employing plans or strata-gems toward a goal. - Merriam-Webster Dictionary

Tactic, 1: a device for accomplishing an end. 2: a method for employing forces in combat. - Merriam-Webster Dictionary

If the strategy is the plan or goal, the tactic is how we implement the plan. The ability to hit the tennis ball consistently in a desired direction is essential to any tactic or strategy. The best planned strategy simply is not of much use if you cannot hit the ball in the desired direction. In other words, developing directional control as well as distance control of the tennis ball is essential to developing strategies that help you win tennis matches.

For more novice players, the goal is to play percentage tennis by hitting every ball cross court. As you work on directional hitting, both down the line and cross court, your confidence will rise and more creative patterns become possible. At this level of play, hitting cross court is a viable tactic in singles as well as in doubles.

When deciding where you should next hit the ball, keep in mind that it is always easiest to return the ball in the direction from which it came. If you are in a cross court rally continue to hit cross court until....

1. Your opponent changes direction of the ball, then continue to hit the ball in the direction from which it came to you. Or you can take the down the line ball from your opponent and go cross court with a higher percentage ball that keeps them moving.

2. Your opponent hits a ball that lands short on your side of the court. This gives you the opportunity to hit the ball as an approach shot and move into the net.

3. Your opponent hits a ball down the middle of the court where you have the opportunity to move around your backhand and hit an inside-out forehand to the opposite corner. This is a more difficult/advanced play but it opens up the angles on the court for an easy winner.

If your opponent has an obvious weak side, by all means play that side as much as possible. Occasionally go to the strong side to keep them honest and to not let them overplay their weak side.

For more novice players, knowing when to play defensively or offensively can be confusing. Keep in mind that if you have time to set up and you feel prepared for the shot, hit it and be offensive. When you feel you are being pushed or are trying to hit the ball while feeling off balance, back off and get a little more air under your shot. Hit it higher and deeper as more of a defensive type shot.

When your opponent seems to be equal on both sides (few players are), be patient and plan to open up the angles on the court by hitting cross court and then down the line and then back cross court. Avoid changing direction of the ball on very deep balls. Don't be afraid to hit back to the same side until you get an opening to change direction. This too is a more advanced tactic.

When you are playing a baseline player who only comes to the net to shake hands, hit more off-speed shots or short-angled balls that bring them to the net. Avoid long baseline rallies with this type of player. Make them play shots and move in a direction that they are less comfortable with.

Singles

For singles play, stay in the moment and focus on each shot to help with timing and control.

○ Have a game plan before you start your match. Then have a back up plan, just in case. This is more difficult than it sounds, particularly if you have never played against your opponent. Try to analyze their play during the warm up and look for strengths and weaknesses. Formulate your game plan before the first serve. If you are lucky enough to have a coach or friend that knows your opponent's game, talk to them and determine what may or may not work. Scouting your opponent is a great way to learn their strengths and weaknesses.

○ When playing a match at whatever your level, feeling butterflies before you play is normal. Use that nervous energy to motivate you to a great start in the match. Organize your thoughts before you play to feel more in control. Warm yourself up. Though it sounds silly, make sure you hit all of the shots you want. Do not let your opponent rush you into starting before you are ready.

○ Hit your groundstrokes with plenty of net clearance and with a lot of balls over the center strap. Intermediate players often have the misconception that a low shot is better but a ball with less net clearance often results in a short ball. The net is a bigger enemy than your opponent so aim high and keep the ball deep. This is especially important at the start of the match. Play your way into feeling comfortable. If you rush, you may be behind sooner than you would like.

○ If you find yourself behind quickly in the match, say 0-3 or 0-4, slow down. Take more time between points and stall a little. Also try some lobs or at least deep, high, slower balls. Do anything to change the rhythm of the match. Slowing the pace of play will get the momentum going in your favor.

○ Stay patient. Don't try to make your first shot a winner. Develop your points. Decide that

you can outlast your opponent with patience. At club level tennis, about 80 percent of all points are lost and 20 percent are won by going for an outright winner. This statistic should encourage you to go for less. Move your targets in a little from the sidelines and the baseline. Raise your sites over the net. Higher net clearance lowers your percentage of unforced errors. Stay consistent.

○ Know your strengths. Practice patterns that force your opponent to play into those strengths. If your forehand is your strength, hit balls that force your opponent to hit to your forehand. Then hit balls to their backhand to force a late contact point so balls comes back down the line to your forehand, opening up the cross court shot for you to win the point. In the past, instructors have discouraged running around your backhand to hit a forehand but if you have time and the correct footwork by all means step around and rip your forehand.

○ Develop your forehand and your backhand so you won't have an obvious weak side. You may always feel stronger on one side, but for successful singles play you need to develop strong shots on both sides. If your forehand is your strength, use it, but don't overlook improving your backhand to a level that equals your forehand.

○ When approaching the net, follow your ball to cover your opponent's best possible angles of return. This is very important in singles since there is more court to cover. Once again, you are playing to cover the percentage response from your opponent.

○ If you lose the point, don't beat yourself up. Nothing works 100 percent of the time. The game wouldn't be much fun if it did. If your opponent hits a great shot, applaud them, even though you may still have done everything right.

○ Center your shots. Hit shots right down the middle of the court to cut down on the angle of your opponent's shot and get you out of trouble. Centering your serve or serving to the body of your opponent reduces the angle of their return. When you run from side to side for shots, try to eliminate the angles by hitting your shot down the middle of the court. This will cut down on your opponent's angles.

○ Mix up the pace. Hit high looping shots that pin your opponent back and get them out of their rhythm. Many times this results in a short ball from your opponent, which is just what you want. Most players don't like off-speed shots. They have to generate pace on the ball to return it. When you hit everything hard, your opponent gets a feel for the timing and returns the ball with more pace, making the rhythm of the swing easy to manage. Try mixing it up, some players hate the off speed stuff. If you play one of them, slow your shots down too. Don't try to slug it out with your opponent.

○ When you are forced out of the court, hit high and deep. The farther you run to get a ball, the higher and deeper you want to make the return. This gives you time to recover and keeps your opponent back, not to mention your percentage of successful returns goes way up. It may also be a more difficult shot for your opponent because of the higher bouncing ball, which is tricky to do much with.

○ Don't get too showy. Cute or low percentage shots often are disastrous. Be the player that won the match not the player who hit one spectacular shot. Play your game.

○ Pay attention to the score. This prevents playing important points without thought. Indeed, all points are important but some of them more so. If you stay in the moment and are aware of the score, you are able to focus more on the important points.

○ Focus on the bounce of the ball. Sound a little crazy? Often we don't focus on the ball until it's time to make the swing. Focusing on the bounce allows you to play the ball not your opponent. This will get you in a better rhythm for your strokes and allow you to adapt your strokes to various speeds and spins more quickly. Getting into the rhythm of the game helps with your timing and focus.

○ Improve your fitness with off-court training. Though fitness is an obvious way to improve, it is often overlooked. I discuss developing an off-court training program in a later chapter.

Doubles

If the only plan a doubles team followed was to hit every ball cross court, that team's success would be very high!

○ Communication is the key to a successful marriage or, for that matter, to any relationship. You and your doubles partner have a relationship. So the more you communicate, the better chance of success you have. Tell your partner: "yours," "mine," "switch." Don't forget to talk between points to let them know where you are trying to serve or if you are attempting to poach.

○ When deciding which side of the court to play, I have always felt the stronger player should play the ad court. The stronger player returns on the bigger points and sets up the net player with a stronger return. If you are right-handed and your partner is left-handed, the feeling is the same. There are arguments both ways as to which player, right or left-handed, should play which side. Keep the stronger player on the ad court!

○ Decide on a plan and stick to it, until it no longer works. It has been said: "never change a winning game but always change a losing game." Words to live by on the tennis court. My coach in college once told me, "There are a lot of ways to lose, you might as well try all of them."

○ Hit to the player who is cross court. Hit deep and keep on them until they miss or you open up the court. If one player on the opposing team stays back, play to that person. Keep them deep and get to the net. This opens up a ton of options for winning the point.

○ Assume every ball is coming to you, except of course when your partner is serving. Be prepared for any shot and by thinking everything is coming back to you, nothing will surprise you.

○ Be deliberate but don't run to the net like a crazy person, but rather work your way in. Make sure you stop or split step when your opponent makes contact with ball. This keeps you from over running your next shot. Most club-level players move too much at the net. Don't get me wrong, you do move your feet to get in position but, stay balanced and controlled and your net game will start to take shape.

○ Find the big green space for winners. The service "T" in the center of the court is a favorite. In other words, play percentage tennis. Don't shoot for a small target. You may find yourself looking at this target instead of concentrating on the ball.

○ Take the pace off the ball when you play against an aggressive net player. Particularly when returning serve, a more softly hit ball is hard to volley, forcing them to hit up. Hitting hard is fun, no question. But change the pace and spin of your shots to make you a much better doubles player. Choose the time to hit the ball hard. If you have a lot of time to set up, hit out. Don't become a pusher, just be a smarter player.

○ Don't look back. If you are the net player, focus on the other side of the court and move in the direction that best covers their movement. There is no need to look back and watch your partner, let them play and focus on the next ball.

○ Placement of your serve is very important. Set up your partner to hit a winner with the first volley. Serve at the body to cut down on sharp angled returns. Though hand signals are often used in advanced doubles, I prefer the net player walk back and talk to their partner. Now the volleyer is ready for the likely placement of the return. Remember that communication is the key to a strong team. Knowing where they intend to serve allows you to better anticipate the angles of your opponents return.

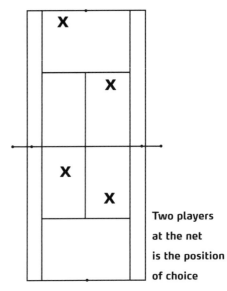

Two players at the net is the position of choice

○ Follow the ball as a team. Shifting one step as a team in the direction of a shot closes off the down the line and middle of the court. This leaves the open area of the court as your opponent's lowest percentage shot. When you shift one step for the first ball, remember you have to shift again after the next shot. Move on every shot. Don't become a spectator, be active.

○ Avoid hanging out in the alley. If you cover the low percentage down the line shot, you leave open the higher percentage, easier-to-hit middle of the court. This forces your partner to cover too much court. Forget the alley unless your opponent frequently and successfully hits down the line. By moving more to the middle of the court, you play "bigger" taking up more space and putting more pressure on your opponent's return.

○ Give yourself a little room. Don't play too close to the net. If you are too close to the net, you lose the ability to move in and cut off volleys and your reaction time is cut down. This results in more defensive and less aggressive play at the net. By playing too close to the net, you are much more susceptible to the lob. Try to position yourself about half way between

the service line and the net. Remember that you can always move in for a softer shot.

○ Observe patterns of play. Patterns in doubles repeat endlessly and geometrically. Observe them and remember them. Anticipate these patterns based on the shot which sets them up, i.e. a serve down the middle creates a volley opportunity for the server's partner. Develop these patterns with your partner and when one pattern works, don't change it. Work it until it no longer works. Your opponents may have shots they like to hit and shots they don't like. This is a pattern. Move to take the favorite shots away and force them to hit shots they don't like to hit. This may be as simple as hitting your first volley down the middle of the court and moving in and hitting a short angled second ball. Use your imagination and hit shots that will open up the court and leave a section of court open for the next ball.

○ Develop and use the lob. This changes the pace of the game and discourages your opponent from lobbing. As discussed earlier, experiment with offensive and defensive lobs. Know when to hit the appropriate type of lob. Also, if you play on a sunny day, lob more often to the side of the court that forces your opponent to look into the sun. Though not really very nice, it is very effective. When you hit a lob that lands very deep, approach the net and stop near the service line. From here, you can cover most of the court and move swiftly to the net for a put away or cover back for deep lob. Very few players can hit an offensive shot from a deep lob, so you are more likely to play offensively.

○ Learn to poach. When playing at the net with your partner back at the baseline, you may poach, or move across the center of the court to intercept a ball hit to your partner. This is a great tactic to keep your opponent off guard. Don't become a spectator, be active. Even if you try to poach and lose the point, it can be a positive by keeping your opponents guessing about where to hit the return.

○ Cover the deep lob. When your opponent lobs over your partner while you are both at the net, it is your responsibility to move back and return the lob. It is much easier for you to hit a solid return off this difficult ball because of your angle of attack. This angle puts you behind where the ball is going to bounce. Let the ball bounce up and come back down. This angle makes your defensive play much easier. As you make this switch to cover the lob, your partner moves to cover the side of the court that was left vacant by the switch, moving back to a neutral area of the court.

○ Play as a team and move to the net together. A team with one up and one back leaves a huge gap in the middle of the court as well as an open area in front of the deep player. Develop and use various formations in your doubles game. Keep changing the look to keep your opponents off guard.

Doubles Formations

Standard one up, one back is the most familiar of all of the formations and what you see most in club tennis. This formation leaves you vulnerable to a ball hit down the middle. It is an inefficient way to cover the court, eliminating a lot of your options when it comes to winning the point.

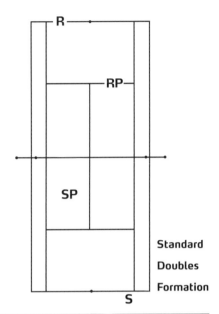

Standard Doubles Formation

Two players at the net is the ideal position. But this requires either a serve and volley strategy or a return and volley. If you are uncomfortable with the serve and volley, be patient and work your way to the net. Be practical and wait for a good approach shot. Use the ball that brings you into the court and follow it in.

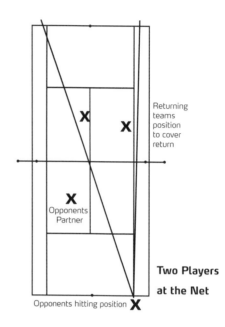

Returning teams position to cover return

X
Opponents Partner

Two Players at the Net

Opponents hitting position X

Two players back is a very defensive position and should only be used if your opponents are very strong and hitting you off the court. It is also effective if you need to change the pace of the game. From the back, you and your partner can use the lob effectively and alter the pace of your shots. Don't plan to stay back for the entire match. When you get a short ball, come in together. Make a quick transition from defense to offense, taking control when you get the chance.

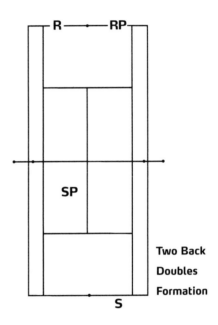

Two Back Doubles Formation

Australian doubles is a great formation if your opponent is ripping cross court returns and the server has a hard time handling the return. Move the net player, the server's partner, to the same side as the server to take away the return your opponent finds most effective. After serving, the server must move across and in to cover the down the line ball.

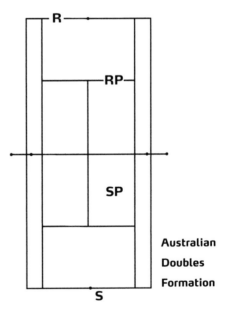

Australian Doubles Formation

The "I" formation is used a lot in top level doubles. The server's partner crouches down straddling the center line of the court. The net player talks to the server and they decide on which direction he/she moves after the serve. This play leads to indecision on the returner's part causing unforced errors on the return.

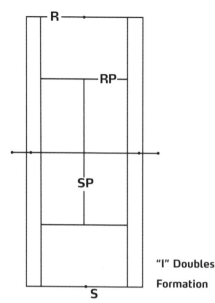

"I" Doubles Formation

With all of the different formations, remember to discuss where each player should move after the serve. Don't end up with both players on the same side of the court. Always keep in mind communication is the key to a great doubles team.

13

CHAPTER

Practice

The legendary golf professional Gary Player once said,

"The more I practice, the luckier I get"

THIS QUOTE RINGS TRUE ON THE TENNIS COURT AS WELL AS THE GOLF COURSE.

Another quote we can apply to our tennis game is, "Practice doesn't make perfect, perfect practice makes perfect." In other words, when you head out to practice, focus. Try to practice all of your shots in a way that improves your overall game. It is unrealistic to think we can play a perfect game of tennis. There are a lot of variables, including the weather, our opponent and our game. By striving to make practice perfect, you can only improve your chances when you step on the court for a match.

You have made a commitment to improve your tennis with instruction, books and videos, but all of it won't help if you don't practice. Establish some goals and discuss them with your coach. Having clear cut goals aids in the learning process and helps avoid frustration. Make your goals, both the long and short term, clear and achievable.

Armed with a solid understanding of how to hit all of the various shots, you can now practice your new skills and ultimately incorporate them into your game.

If you are alone, don't panic. You have plenty of options to practice your tennis. You can improve your strokes and work on conditioning in a couple of ways.

Practicing Alone

A ball machine is the best way to incorporate a new skill into your game or to work out a bad habit. This machine simply throws balls to you so you can practice a specific stroke or shot, with no pressure to hit the ball back to a person or to a specific spot on the court. This frees you up to experiment with the stroke. Avoid setting the machine to throw too fast or too quickly, as it may be frustrating. Take it slow, focusing on the changes you want to incorporate into your game. Some machines oscillate, by throwing the ball from side to side. Don't let your ego get in the way by trying to run from corner to corner. That may sound a little confusing. Use the ball machine to work on your strokes, try not to be the macho player that has to run after every ball. You can't beat the machine. Use the ball machine with a friend too, one hits and one picks up, then change places.

When a partner can't be found, try a backboard. It can also be very frustrating. So focus on being as consistent as possible. If you over hit or hit too hard, most of your time will be spent picking up balls. Be patient and work your strokes and footwork, not your power. This is also a very effective way to work on your volleys. Start about 8-10 feet from the

wall and volley as long as you can keep the ball going. Hit only forehand volleys and then only backhand volleys. As you progress, try to alternate between the two. This cuts down the shoulder turn and simplifies the volley on both sides. Be creative and have fun.

Practice with a Partner

When using a progressive warm up, start slowly. Mini-tennis is a favorite of mine. From opposite service lines gently stroke the ball back and forth using both backhands and forehands. The secret to hitting softly is to shorten your swing. The closer you get to the net, the shorter your backswing. After a few minutes of mini-tennis, move back to the middle of the court to "no-man's land." Now you will have to hit half-volleys and groundstrokes to keep the rally alive. By lengthening the swing, try to have the ball to bounce on the opposite service line.

Then move to the baseline. Use a full swing but not full speed. Start with only about 75% of your maximum pace. Remember you are still warming up. Keep your feet moving and work on control. Pay special attention to the contact point in the swing.

As you start to get a rhythm on your strokes, begin to hit in a direction. First with cross court forehands and then backhands. Keep the ball in play and begin to increase the pace just a little while staying consistent. Don't forget to hit down the line as well. Try alternating forehand and backhand shots. This increases the number of steps between shots, improving your footwork.

To increase the intensity of the drill, have your partner stay in the forehand half of the court and hit down the line then cross court. You move side to side, directing your shots back to your partner. After a few minutes, switch having your partner move side to side so you both have to run. Make sure you hit balls to both sides of he court. To really get your heart going, hit down the line and have your partner hit cross court so both of you move side to side. Make sure you switch directions, ensuring you both practice hitting all of the shots. Have a great workout! Don't over hit. These are consistency drills.

These patterns are also great with one player at the net and one at the baseline. Keep working on directional control and depth.

Practice with Three Players

While waiting for a fourth to show for doubles, there are a myriad of drills to explore. The old stand by two-on-one drill has a lot of variations. Here are a few.

1. Two-on-one from the baseline. All players are back with a doubles team on one baseline and the singles player on the other. The doubles players hit down the line while the singles player hits cross court. A good workout for the singles player is maintaining steadiness to keep the rally going. For increased intensity, have the doubles players hit cross court and the singles player hit down the line. Keep rotating around so no one is left out of the running. This very simple drill is super for working on changing the direction of the ball. Vary the drill by keeping the singles player on one side. The doubles players only hit to that side. Play this as a groundstroke game but attack any short ball and go to net. Both teams work the transition

from the baseline to the net with their split step. Keep score as it keeps everyone focused. Try playing games to ten, play both sides and rotate around.

2. Two at the net, one on the baseline. Have the two volleyers hit for the singles court and the baseline player hit to the doubles court. Play this drill for control or play out points. Keeping score is a great way to stay motivated. Either way this is a fun drill that works your entire game.

3. Two at the baseline one at the net. This is a variation of the previous drill. Throw in some lobs for variety or limit lobbing to build consistency on the groundstrokes.

Practice with Four Players

When most players head on the court, they warm up for five or ten minutes and are ready to take some serves. Instead, extend the warm up making it a practice session.

1. Hit in all of the directions, cross court forehands and backhands from the baseline and with two players at the net. Hit some lobs and overheads. Literally hit all the shots. Spend five to ten minutes hitting in each direction, don't forget down the line groundstrokes and volleys.

2. Have some fun playing volley points. Two players start on each service line hitting volleys and playing out the point. Close in after each shot and play this without letting the ball bounce. It's very fast and a lot of fun. Keep score to make everyone focus a bit more. Try games to seven or ten points.

3. Move two players back to the baseline and play some points with two up and two back. Eliminate the bounce for the net team and allow anything goes for the baseline team. This is a great drill to sharpen the skills needed in doubles.

4. Start with all four players back and rally until one team gets a short ball to attack and finish the point at net. This is great for working the depth of your groundstrokes and understanding when to attack the short ball.

5. Be creative. Make up your own drills to work on your weak shots. If you are a doubles player, try to work most of the drill cross court and come in to the net. There are endless possibilities when it comes to ways to practice. Most of all, have fun.

Getting in Shape for Tennis

Tennis is a great way to develop your overall fitness. Implementing an off-court training program can help lift the level of your game. If you are more fit and don't change anything in your game, you will play better and for a longer period of time. As with any fitness program, consult your physician before beginning a new program.

To get the most bang for your workout buck, consult with a certified personal trainer. They can develop a program that is sport specific and geared to improving your tennis game.

Tennis is a unique sport that is primarily an anaerobic activity. The short bursts of activity require quicker movements for shorter periods of time. Increasing your aerobic fitness will greatly reduce your recovery time between points. It also improves your endurance for those long, three-set matches.

Overall fitness is the goal with the target of improving your tennis game. Let's look at all of the options from quickness and strength training to aerobic fitness and stretching.

Strength Training doesn't necessarily mean throwing around heavy weights. A better option may be lighter weights with more repetitions being the goal. We want to build strength and endurance, not bulk. Iso-metric resistance bands, the thick rubber band device you

may have seen in the gym, are bands that stretch and will add resistance to a given exercise. Stretch the resistance band and hold it for a given period of time and then release. This sounds simple but it is very effective. Also, good old fashioned push-ups are a fantastic way to increase your strength. Your personal trainer can show you many variations for the push up, depending on your strength.

Quickness Drills are designed to improve quickness and first-step speed. In tennis, you never need to run a mile, but how quick you make the first step or two is ultimately important. A jump rope will also help to increase foot speed. It's not only for little kids. It's fun and will help your footwork.

Cardio Training is designed to keep your heart rate in its target zone for a minimum of 20 minutes. Cardiovascular exercise increases the oxygen in the blood stream and aids in recovery between long points. Some examples of cardiovascular exercises are biking, elliptical trainers, stair-climbing machines and jogging. It is a good idea to use a heart rate monitor as this will help ensure your heart rate is in the target zone for the optimum training benefit. Avoid a lot of bone jarring activities that may cause joint pain. Tennis is jarring enough so save your knees as much as possible.

Core Strength is the strength of the muscles in your core area, abdominals, lower back and oblique muscles. These muscle groups are all tied together and incorporated in almost all tennis shots. Increased strength through crunches, planking and medicine-ball training increases your strength and stamina in this important area of the body.

Stretching and staying flexible is important for all ages but even more important as we start to age. Improved flexibility helps avoid injury and increases rotational speed in almost all of our tennis strokes.

Find the right fitness program for your needs and make the available time to work out. A trained fitness professional can help explain all of these ideas. The value of a good fitness and strength program is proven when you easily hit the court and take a set from a worthy opponent. There are a lot of good tennis specific books on training available. If you don't have access to a personal trainer, look for one of these books.

14

CHAPTER

Equipment

NOW THAT YOU HAVE YOUR GAME IN SHAPE, LET'S TALK ABOUT YOUR EQUIPMENT.

There are literally hundreds of racquets on the market today and people ask me all the time which racquet is best for their game. If a racquet manufacturer is in business today, they are making a good product. Each company has their own claim to fame when it comes to technology and they all seem to change every other year or so.

First and foremost, don't buy a new racquet because you see your favorite player using it on TV. Most likely, it has been customized for your hero and is very different from the racquet you may buy. The professional players you see need all of their racquets to be exactly the same because a few grams of extra weight can make a difference in their performance. Equally as important, don't buy a racquet because your friend likes it. Finally, don't buy a racquet off the wall of a chain or sporting goods store because a salesman tells you it is the hottest new thing on the market. They probably have too many of them in stock and are just trying to get rid of a particular model.

When looking into buying a new racquet, there are several things to consider:

1. Match the racquet to your particular swing. Someone with a long fast swing should use a more flexible racquet than a player with a short slower swing. A racquet with a wider/thicker beam is stiffer, making it more powerful. A thinner beam is more flexible, thus less powerful. The difference can be huge and playing with the wrong racquet may make you change your swing and possibly cause arm problems.

2. Racquet weight. The way a racquet feels in your hand when you are just holding it is the static weight, which means an eight ounce, head-heavy racquet feels heavier than a 9.5 ounce racquet that is balanced more light in the head. This becomes more evident when you swing the racquet. Swing weight is harder to measure but easy to feel when you start making your strokes with a particular weight and balanced racquet.

3. Weight translates to power. The heavier your racquet, the more power – that is if you can keep the swing speed the same. The more mass behind the impact of the swing, the less shock there will to your arm. If you have arm problems, you may consider a slightly heavier frame which seems opposite of what you may think. Try a little lead tape, but don't go crazy adding it to your racquet. Try a little and see how it feels. It is a case of a little goes a long way. Adding lead to different areas of the head of the racquet changes the position of the sweet spot on the frame. The sweet spot is the point on the strings where the least vibration occurs when striking the ball. See your local professional for more advice on where to add weight.

4. Grip Size. The easiest way to see if your grip is the correct size is to hold the racquet in your dominate hand and place the index finger of your non-dominate hand between your fingers and the fleshy part of your thumb. If you play with a grip that is too small your wrist will be looser and harder to keep firm, especially on the volleys. If your grip is too large, you may have trouble releasing your wrist on the serve and overhead. Your grip may become fatigued much more quickly, diminishing your ability to control the racquet.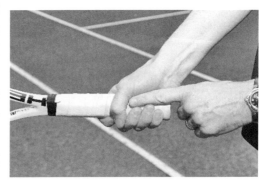

5. When you do find a racquet you love, take care of it. Don't leave it in your car, the heat and humidity cause havoc on the strings.

To purchase a racquet, go to a reputable dealer and ask about the demo policy. After you decide on a few racquets to try based on your swing speed, the weight and balance of the racquet and how comfortable it feels to you, ask if you can take three or four racquets out to the courts and try each of them for five or ten minutes. By trying several racquets at one time, you can weed out the models that you don't like right away. Go back to the shop and explain which ones you liked and disliked and see if they have others that may be a fit. Try the ones you like the best on another day and then make a decision. Be patient. With so many options, you don't want to buy

the wrong racquet. Quality racquets can cost up to $300. Don't panic as there are many quality choices for much less. Keep in mind that you plan to use your new racquet a lot (hopefully) so try not to let price influence your buying decision.

String

If there are hundreds of racquets, there are twice as many types of string. Don't fret, let's narrow it down. Since the string is the only part of the racquet that touches the ball (we hope), it is important that we just don't ask for whatever is cheapest. Try to find what is best for your game. Most shops have a variety of string to choose from. Ask the sales person for help and describe your game. If you tend to break strings frequently or have arm trouble, your choice is more important. String is available in a variety of materials, thicknesses (gauges), colors and prices.

Natural Gut

Natural gut is not from cats but from the serosa portion of a cow intestine. About three cows are needed to make a set of string for one tennis racquet. The intestine is stripped, wound, stretched and coated to make tennis string. It is the best playing string on the market with the softest feel and is the easiest on your arm. It plays exceptionally well until it breaks. Even though it is the most expensive string you can buy, many players swear that it is worth every penny. Although the coatings used on natural gut are far superior than in the past, it is still a good idea to avoid playing with gut string in the rain. Even a light mist can shorten the life of your strings.

Synthetics

This is the widest range of performance, durability and playability, from the very inexpensive synthetic gut, which has nothing to do with natural gut, to the super soft multifilament synthetics that claim to play like natural gut. Some have a monofilament core with a wrap on the outside. Some are true multifilament, made up of thousands of strands of nylon. The more strands of nylon, the softer the string plays. If you have any arm problems, consider a much softer string. Prices run the extreme from inexpensive to almost the price of natural gut. The low end of the synthetics can be less than half the price of natural gut. Remember, no one plays tennis to save money. If a more expensive string can help improve your game or help alleviate some of your arm pain, don't scrimp on the price of your string.

Polyester

Though it has been around a long time, polyester string has recently become popular with hard hitting juniors and top professionals. It is a monofilament string that is firm when the ball strikes the string bed. It is also very durable and it is very hard to break. That is one of the reasons the hardest hitting players love this string. A lot of professional players are now playing with what is called hybrid string, polyester in the main strings and a soft synthetic or natural gut in the crosses, or vice versa. The down side of polyester string is that it goes dead very quickly. If you are a pro player and have your racquets strung every week, it's a good choice. It is not a good choice for everyone, especially the players with elbow or shoulder problems.

The Gauge or Thickness of the String

The thickness of the string you choose determines several things, most important is the feel the string has in the racquet. The other is how long the string lasts. Standard string ranges from 15 gauge as the thickest to 18 gauge as the thinnest; most shops sell 16 and 17 gauge. If you are a string breaker, go thicker. If you have never broken a string, you may want to go thinner. The thinner the string, the more feel you will have when the ball strikes the string bed. If you have had some arm troubles, try a thinner gauge string. Most players feel they can get more spin on their shots with a thinner string, but there is no scientific evidence for these claims.

Tension

Quite simply, the tighter the string, the more "control" you have. Conversely, the looser the strings, the more "power" is generated by the string bed. The weather can effect your string tension so if you play in extremely hot conditions, you may want your racquet strung a couple of pounds tighter. This is also true if you are playing in higher altitudes. If you change racquets, the tension that feels the best in the new racquet may not be the same as the old one. Experiment a pound or two in either direction to achieve the feel you want in the new racquet. The minute a racquet comes off the stringing machine it begins to loose tension. Polyester string loses tension the fastest and natural gut the slowest. Synthetic strings lose tension at various rates depending on the make up of the string. This is known as the creep factor. When restringing, you may want to add a couple of pounds to the string job to have it come out where you feel the most comfortable.

When to Restring

The United States Racquet Stringer Association recommends the number of times you play a week as the number of times you should restring your racquet in a year. So the rule of thumb in the industry today is if you play twice a week, you should restring twice a year. Obviously, if you break a string or your strings feel soft, by all means, restring. Tension loss is gradual so you may be playing with a racquet that has lost too much tension and you have just become accustomed to it.

Grips

Only a few racquets come with leather grips in today's market. Some old school players still like the harder, tacky feel of a real leather grip. Most of us use a synthetic/rubber compound grip. They do wear out, sometimes rather quickly. If your grip starts to show signs of wear or starts to become slippery, it is time for a change. Remember it is the only contact you have with the racquet when you are playing. Mind your grip and you will have more control on the racquet.

Over Grips

A thin wrap that is added over the existing grip is an overgrip. Some overgrips are quite tacky and give a sticky feel to the grip while others have a more of a felt-like quality. Both styles are good and it comes to personal preference. It does add about 1/16" to the size of your grip. These too wear out. Replace them as often as necessary.

Shoes

Each tennis shoe manufacturer makes shoes for a variety of courts - grass, hard and clay. You don't have to go crazy with your footwear but find a shoe that is comfortable and designed for the type of court you play on most frequently. As with racquets, don't buy a shoe because your favorite player is wearing it. All shoes are made on different lasts and fit differently. Find a quality shoe that fits. Try on both shoes and wear them around the shop for a little while to see if they both fit comfortably before you make a purchase.

For the most part, your insoles and cushioning wear out before you wear through the sole, especially if you play on clay or soft courts. Make sure you are not wearing a pair of shoes that has lost cushioning. Buy two pair of shoes that you like and alternate them if you play a lot of tennis.

Do not wear running shoes or cross trainers to play tennis. They are designed for running and training with the heal of the shoe built up for a forward slant, which is very comfortable for running and for the heel strike. They are very unstable and very easy to roll an ankle with the side to side movement of tennis. Most clubs discourage cross-trainers or running shoes that have black or dark soles that can mark hard courts with black streaks. Many clubs do not allow these shoes on their hard courts either indoor or outdoor.

What's in your Tennis Bag

Your racquet bag isn't just for getting your racquets from your car to the courts. Make sure you carry the essentials you may need during or after your match.

Sunscreen: Use a high SPF sunscreen and reapply during the change over of a match. No matter the claim, it does sweat off.

A visor, hat or baseball cap: This is a great help if you're serving into the sun.

An extra shirt, or two: Changing from your sweaty shirt during or immediately after a match can make you feel much more comfortable.

Insect repellent: In some areas, bugs can be annoying at best and a definite distraction so don't be afraid to use repellent. Be careful to avoid getting repellent in your eyes.

A towel: Pack an extra hand towel to dry off your hands, grip and face during a match.

Water and extra water bottle: Bring an energy drink or water. Have extras in your bag. Drinking more liquids than you need is better than becoming dehydrated.

An energy bar or banana: Having a little snack for the longer matches can be a big help in maintaining your energy level.

Wristbands and headbands: Pack an extra pair or two when they do become wet a quick change can help keep your hands and head dry.

Extra over grips: If your grip gets too slippery during a match, change the over grip.

A notebook: Make some notes on your opponents. This can also be helpful to keep notes on your game as a reminder of key thoughts during the match.

Tennis and Travel

YOU'VE DECIDED ON A TENNIS VACATION.....

Going on a tennis vacation may be more work and more fun than you expect. Here are some things to consider before and during your trip to tennis school.

Do some research and find the tennis school that best fits your needs. There are a few schools with great reputations. Some resorts offer other activities for the non-tennis members of your group and may be fun for you after your tennis sessions.

Don't expect too much: Tennis school is a lot of fun but if your expectations are too high, you may leave a bit frustrated. At school, you receive a lot of information in a short period of time. Pick a few tips to focus on and incorporate them into your game. Even the best instruction takes some practice to become second nature. Be patient with your improvements.

Prepare: I know it sounds silly but play a few extra times before going on your tennis vacation to get your body ready for five or six hours on the court. Make sure you play in regulation tennis shoes and have played in them a few times before you go. New shoes can be painful with all of the running you do at camp. Do not wear running or cross training shoes. They are dangerous on a tennis court and some resorts discourage them on the soft (clay) courts. See more on footwear in the equipment section.

Pack for a variety of weather conditions. Make sure you have a warm-up suit or sweatshirt in case the weather turns cool. Also, pack extra shirts and socks. You are bound to work up a sweat so having a dry shirt makes the afternoon much more comfortable. Change your socks to keep your feet dry and help prevent blisters.

Obviously bring plenty of sunscreen. Wear a hat and sunglasses when spending a full day in the sun. Also wearing a hat and sunglasses can help prevent headaches when you are outside all day.

Be honest about your ability: If the camp asks about your level of play, be honest. You may think you play better when you play with more experienced players but since you usually play with people your own level, it makes sense to practice at that level also. A group of players at your same level makes the drills more realistic. If by chance you get into a group that is either too high or too low, talk to the pro on your court and nicely ask if there may be a way to change groups. The staff will do everything they can to make sure you are in the right place. Also, if you are working too hard or not hard enough don't wait until the last minute to say something. Mention it to the pro on your court. They should be able to adjust the pace of the group. The school or camp may ask for your NTRP rating, which is the National Tennis Rating Program that the United Stated Tennis Association has developed. The NTRP is series of numbers from 1.0 a beginner to 7.0 a tour professional. The intermediate player is usually between a 3.0 and 4.0 level.

Arrive a few minutes early: By arriving early, the staff of the school has adequate time to make sure everyone is checked in and the groups are ready to go on time. Take this time to inform the staff of any special needs or requests you have before the school starts. The extra time also allows you to get the lay of the land and see what off court activities are available. A massage or a trip to the hot tub may be a great way to end the day.

On the court: Be patient, it is a long day. Most sessions start with a light warm up to get the kinks out and get a feel for the courts. This also lets you meet the other players in your group. You may hear some techniques and tips that aren't the same as your pro at home. Keep an open mind and try the new techniques. You didn't come to camp to hear your game is perfect. Some of these may work and feel comfortable right away and some may not but try it and remember that it is always fun to learn new things.

Use your time wisely. When picking up balls ask questions. Ask your pro specific things about their instruction. Just make sure you still pick up your share of the balls.

Take notes: There is a lot of information thrown at you in a couple of days so don't try to remember all of it. Write things down. A great time for note taking is during the video analysis. Ask questions and listen. You may also find the tips given to other members of your group can help clarify some the changes you want to make.

Terminology

Ace: *Any serve that lands in the service box and is not touched by the returner.*

Advantage: *The point following deuce, the player/team with the advantage has game point.*

Ad Court: *The side of the court where one team has the advantage, also called the backhand side of the court.*

> **Ad In:** *When the server has the advantage*
>
> **Ad Out**: *When the returner has the advantage*

Alley: *The area of the court that is between the singles sideline and the doubles sideline, also called the tramline.*

Approach Shot: *A shot that is made after the ball bounces and the player making the shot moves forward to the net area of the court.*

Approach Volley: *A shot that is made after the ball bounces and the player making the shot moves in toward the net area of the court.*

Association of Tennis Professionals, ATP: *The governing body for men's professional tennis.*

Australian Formation: *A doubles formation where the server and his/her partner start the point on the same side of the court.*

Backhand: *A shot is made on the left side of a right-handed player.*

Backspin/Slice: *A ball that is rotating or spinning underneath itself while traveling forward.*

Backswing: *The backward movement of the racquet that sets up the forward swing.*

Baseline: *The end line on both side of the court.*

Bevel: *The flat panels on the handle of the racquet.*

Break Serve/Break Point: *Winning the game when your opponent is serving or when the returning player has a game point on the opponents serve.*

Cardio Training: *A training method which keeps the heart rate at an elevated level for a designated period of time.*

Center Mark: *The small mark in the middle of the baseline on the court.*

Center "T": *The point of the court where the center service land the service line intersect.*

Changeover/Changeover Time: *When players change ends of the court usually after each odd numbered game.*

Closed Racquet Face: *When the hitting face or side of the racquet is turned down toward the court.*

Closed Stance: *When the front foot crosses the plane of the back foot, usually when referring to the groundstrokes.*

Contact Point: *The point in the swing where the racquet makes contact with the ball.*

Continental Grip: *Or the hammer grip usually used for the serves, volley and overheads.*

Counter Puncher: *A baseline player who specializes in a defensive style of play, sometimes called a backboard.*

Cross Court: *Any shot that is hit diagonally on the court, opposite of hitting down the line.*

Davis Cup: *An international team competition for men. Played each year with the winning countries progressing to a head to head final.*

Deuce: *The score when both players or teams have each won three points in a game.*

Deuce side: *The side of the court to the left of the server for right handed players.*

Double Fault: *When the server has missed both the first and second serves resulting in loss of the point.*

Doubles Sideline: *The lines on the outside of the court to the right and to the left.*

Drop Shot: *A touch shot that is played off the bounce and barely falls over the net usually with some underspin and bounce many times before reaching the service line.*

Drop Step: *The first step when preparing to hit an overhead.*

Drop Volley: *Similar to a drop shot but is played as a volley.*

Drive: *Usually groundstrokes that are hit with power after the bounce.*

Eastern Backhand Grip: *The grip of choice for most one-handed backhand players.*

Eastern Forehand Grip: *Referred to as the handshake grip, used for many types of fore-hands.*

End Change: *When players change ends of the court, same as changeover.*

Flat: *A ball that is hit with little or no spin.*

Fault: *A serve that is hit and does not go in the correct service box or goes into the net.*

Federation Cup: *An international team event for women. Played each year with the winning countries progressing to a head-to-head final.*

Follow Through: *The finish of a swing, or the part of the swing that happens after the contact point.*

Foot Fault: *When the server touches the baseline or court before making contact with the ball, same result as missing the serve.*

Forcing Shot: *A shot that forces your opponent into a defensive position or to make an error.*

Game: *The first to win four points by a two point margin, six games make a set.*

Grip: *The part of the racquet that you hold onto; also this can describe the way you hold the racquet.*

Grand Slam: *Winning all of the four major tournaments in one calendar year, the Australian, the French, Wimbledon and the U.S. Open.*

Groundstroke: *Any forehand or backhand that is made after the ball bounces.*

Half Volley: *A ball that is hit right off the bounce while it is still on the rise.*

Hitting Zone: *The ideal position in the swing where the racquet strikes the ball.*

Hold Serve: *When the server wins the game he/she is serving*

High Percentage Shot: *The choice of shots that has the highest probability of landing in the court.*

"I" Formation: *A doubles formation where the net player starts low in the center of the court and moves with the serve.*

Let Serve: *A serve that hits the top of the net and goes in the correct service box, the serve is replayed.*

Lob: *A groundstroke that is hit high over the net players head.*
    Lob Volley: *Same as a lob but is hit before the ball bounces.*

Loop Backswing: *A "C" shaped backswing that starts high and loops to a position lower than the contact point.*

Love: *A term used in score keeping when a player has no points.*

Low Percentage Shot: *The choice of shots that has the lowest probability of landing in the court.*

Match: *Usually the best two-out-of-three sets except in Grand Slam tournaments and Davis Cup where the men play three-out-of-five sets.*

Net Cord: *When a ball hits the top of the net and goes in the court*

No-Ad Scoring: *A system of scoring where at three points all, the next point wins the game.*

On the Rise: *Hitting the ball as it comes off the court while it is still rising or coming up.*

On Serve: *Where both players continue to win their own service games.*

Open Racquet Face: *The racquet face is turned up or toward the sky.*

Open Stance: *A position for hitting groundstrokes where the front foot has not crossed over the plane of the back foot.*

Out: *Any shot that lands outside the lines of the court.*

Overhead/Smash: *An overhead swinging motion similar to a service motion that takes place during a point.*

Over Grip: *A thin material that wraps over the permanent grip to prevent slipping and absorb or wick moisture.*

Passing Shot: *A groundstroke used to hit past an opponent either at the net or coming into the net.*

Percentage Tennis: *A style of play that incorporates the easiest and safest shots with the highest probability of landing in the court.*

Poaching: *A doubles tactic when the net player moves across the court and intercepts a ball heading for their partner.*

Rally: *When two players hit the ball back and forth over the net, usually hitting ground-strokes.*

Ready Position: *The athletic position used when waiting for your opponent's shot prior to moving for the ball.*

Return or return of serve: *When a player hits the ball back from an opponents serve.*

Round Robin Tournament: *A tournament format where groups of players play everyone in their group, advancing to a final group or pairing.*

Semi-Western Grip: *A type of grip used to hit a forehand where the hand is positioned to the back side of the handle of the racquet.*

Serve: *The shot used to start the point usually an overhead swing.*

Serve + Volley: *Hitting the serve and immediately advancing to the net to hit the return as a volley.*

Service Box: *The area of the court where the serve must land to be considered a good serve.*

Service Line: *The line across the middle of the court that designated the back of the service box.*

Set: *A designation of scoring that represents a set is the first player to win six games by a margin of two.*

    Pro Set: *First to win ten games by a margin of two, designed to speed up play.*

Singles Sideline: The sideline of the court that designates the singles court.

Slice or underspin: *When the ball spins backwards while going through the air or any shot that makes the ball spin backwards.*

Split step or check step: *The stopping step to ready a player coming in to net usually made when the opponent is hitting the return.*

Straight Backswing: *Taking the backswing portion of the swing straight back to the position before the forward swing.*

Sweet Spot: *The area of the face of the racquet where the least vibration occurs usually in the center of the racquet.*

Swing Path: *The plane or angle of the racquet during the forward swing takes place.*

Swing Speed: *How fast the racquet moves during the forward motion of the swing.*

Tie Breaker: *Scoring method used when the set score is 6-6, when this is used the set is not won by two games.*

Topspin: *When the ball is going through the air the ball is spinning forward.*

Toss: *The lifting of the ball with the non-dominate hand, placing the ball in the air for the overhead service motion.*

Touch Shot: *Refers to any shot that requires soft hands and a feel for the ball to hit it the appropriate distance.*

Two-Handed Backhand: *A backhand stroke made with both hands on the racquet.*

Unforced Error: *An error on a swing that is a routine stroke with no pressure.*

United States Professional Tennis Association, USPTA: *One of two governing bodies for the tennis teaching professional.*

United Stated Racquet Stringers Association, USRSA: *The governing body for racquet stringers and technicians.*

United States Tennis Association, USTA: *The governing body for tennis in the United States.*

Volley: *Any ball that is hit before it bounces, excluding the serve and overhead.*

Volley Position: *The position on the court near the net where the volley is hit most effectively.*

Warm Up: *The time prior to the start of the match, used to get ready for the start of a match.*

Western Grip: *A type of forehand grip where the hand is turned under the racquet handle.*

Winner: *A shot that is un-returnable by the opponent.*

Women's Tennis Association, WTA: *The governing body for women's professional tennis.*

Acknowledgments

PUTTING THIS BOOK TOGETHER WAS A TEAM EFFORT. I WOULD LIKE TO THANK Liza Horan, who without her help, this would never had happened. I also want to thank Randy Walker and his staff at New Chapter Press for publishing the book, Cynthia Lum for the exceptional photographs, Lance Jeffrey for the sequential photographs, Chris Rogers and Ralf Reinecke for their photography, Curtis McCarthy and Sandy Malcolm for the local photo shoots, Bob Schule who pushed me to finish this project, Sally Larkin who helped me with the early edits, Jill Powers for her help with the court diagrams, Sean Keith, Jeff Werder, Tory Manchester, Dana Stewart and Tyler Nowakowski for their help with the photos, to Jason "Squid" Stokes for being a great friend, and to Joan Teaford for her help with everything.

Tennis Without Borders

ONE HUNDRED PERCENT OF THE PROFITS ON SALES OF *TENNIS MADE EASY* WILL BE CONTRIBUTED to *Tennis Without Borders*, a not-for-profit organized to help students in third world countries pursue life opportunities on and off court by providing gear, instructions and academic support to clubs and schools.

Tennis Without Borders started in 2002 when Kelly Gunterman and Joan Teaford traveled to Uganda. The tennis-teaching couple accepted an invitation to help instruct children, train school and club staff, and practice with Uganda's Davis Cup team. The learning experience off the court was powerful.

"Everyone was so eager to learn the game and to improve," said Gunterman. "It didn't seem to matter that they were playing with old balls and racquets with broken strings."

Gunterman devoted himself to building awareness and collecting resources for communities from Africa to South America where tennis passion is plentiful, but tennis resources are not. *Tennis Without Borders* received its 501(c)3 status in July 2009 and accepts contributions of cash and gifts-in-kind of tennis equipment. Donations are tax-deductible.

To contribute, individuals can make a financial contribution toward the purchase of equipment, instruction and academic opportunities. A check can be sent, payable to *Tennis Without Borders*, to;

Tennis WithOut Borders
1927 S. Fletcher Ave.
Fernandina Beach, Fla. 32034

Tennis Manufacturers + Retailers can make an in-kind gift of string, balls, racquets or soft goods, or a financial contribution.

For more information, email Kelly Gunterman at guntermank@gmail.com or go to www.GreatTennis.com

Also From New Chapter Press

THE EDUCATION OF A TENNIS PLAYER–By Rod Laver and Bud Collins

Rod Laver's first-hand account of his historic 1969 Grand Slam sweep of all four major tennis titles is documented in this memoir, written by Laver along with co-author and tennis personality Bud Collins. The book details his childhood, early career and his most important matches. The four-time Wimbledon champion and the only player in tennis history to win two Grand Slams also sprinkles in tips and lessons on how players of all levels can improve their games. Originally published in 1971, *The Education of a Tennis Player* was updated in 2009 on the 40th anniversary of his historic second Grand Slam with new content, including the story of his recovery from a near-fatal stroke in 1998.

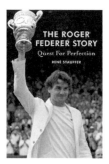

THE ROGER FEDERER STORY, QUEST FOR PERFECTION–By Rene Stauffer

Regarded by many as the greatest tennis player in the history of the sport, this authoritative biography is based on many exclusive interviews with Federer and his family as well as the author's experience covering the international tennis circuit for many years. Completely comprehensive, it provides an informed account of the Swiss tennis star from his early days as a temperamental player on the junior circuit, through his early professional career, to his winning major tennis tournaments, including the U.S. Open and Wimbledon. Readers will appreciate the anecdotes about his early years, revel in the insider's view of the professional tennis circuit, and be inspired by this champion's rise to the top of his game.

THE BUD COLLINS HISTORY OF TENNIS–By Bud Collins

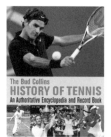

Compiled by the most famous tennis journalist and historian in the world, this book is the ultimate compilation of historical tennis information, including year-by-year recaps of every tennis season, biographical sketches of every major tennis personality, as well as stats, records, and championship rolls for all the major events. The author's personal relationships with major tennis stars offer insights into the world of professional tennis found nowhere else.

www.NewChapterMedia.com